DECORATIVE BEADED PURSES

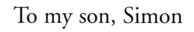

To my son, Simon

DECORATIVE
BEADED
PURSES

ENID TAYLOR

GUILD OF MASTER CRAFTSMAN PUBLICATIONS LTD

First published 1999 by
Guild of Master Craftsman Publications Ltd
166 High Street, Lewes, East Sussex BN7 1XU

Reprinted 2000 (twice), 2001, 2002, 2003

ISBN 1 86108 143 X

Photographs by Gavin Mist
Illustrations and charts by Simon Rodway based on charts
created by Enid and Terry Taylor

A catalogue record for this book is available from the
British Library

Designed by Fran Rawlinson
Typeface: Adobe Garamond
Colour origination by Viscan Graphics (Singapore)
Printed and bound by Kyodo Printing (Singapore)

ACKNOWLEDGEMENTS
I would like to thank Caroline Crabtree of World
Embroidery Supplies and Jill Devon of The Bead Merchant
for their advice on beads. My thanks also to Gavin Mist for
his expertise and patience in producing the photographs;
it is always a pleasure to work with him. I would like to
record my special thanks to my husband, Terry, for his
patience and help throughout the production of the book.
I am especially grateful for his skill in converting my
designs to make the charts for my purses.

CONTENTS

INTRODUCTION

Beads have been used throughout history, from ancient times to the present day, and by all civilisations, from the Aztecs to the Zulus.

The original meaning of the word bead, or bede, was a prayer. Beads were used for centuries for religious rites, and are still used in the form of the rosary. They were believed to ward off evil spirits and were worn around the neck or on the arm. The more beads worn the greater the protection afforded, so necklaces and bracelets are relics of old superstitions as well as being used for decoration and adornment.

The use of beads in embroidery is subject to changes in fashion. In Elizabethan times, purses were richly decorated with gold thread and beads. Beadwork grew in popularity throughout the seventeenth century, but fell out of favour in the eighteenth century. By the early years of the nineteenth century it came into vogue again; both knitted and woven beaded purses were particularly popular. Small purses were worn as necklaces and regarded by some as good luck charms. They were also used to hold charms or amulets, from precious stones to slips of parchment inscribed with passages of religious law.

The popularity of beadwork this century has fluctuated. After the 1920s, when dresses made almost entirely of beads were the height of fashion, there was a loss of interest, but the use of beads in embroidery has become more widespread in recent years. Beaded purses have once again become popular and this has meant rediscovering and learning old skills.

My students wished to make these purses and, with their encouragement, I have attempted to gather together the instructions used in our workshops. I have not touched upon the delightful purses which can be made by knitting yarn threaded with beads. I have confined myself to stitched purses and a few small accessories which use the basic stitches employed in making the purses.

The basic stitch information is contained in the first three chapters, the patterns for the purses and other items which feature later in the book will refer you back to the techniques you need.

Chapter 1

MATERIALS AND EQUIPMENT

Only a small amount of equipment is needed for making beaded purses: scissors, a thimble, a tape measure, special beading needles, a pad to work on, storage units for the beads and a small pair of pliers. The materials needed are simply beads and thread.

Needles

The holes in the beads used to make these purses are small. For some designs, e.g. those which use square stitch, the thread passes several times through the beads, consequently the holes can become full. It is therefore advisable to use fine needles for beading work.

Specialist beading needles come in a variety of sizes and lengths. I find that the long size 10 suits me best. It can be easily threaded and its long length makes it suitable for picking up individual beads, and for threading through a long row of beads.

The finer size 13 needle is useful when beads get too full of thread, or for beads with exceptionally small holes. You may find you need a magnifying glass to thread this size of needle. Another disadvantage of this size is that it bends easily and the needle or the eye will break if put under a lot of pressure.

Embroidery shops often sell multi-sized packs of beading needles. As time goes by you will find that you need to replace the size 10s, which you will use most frequently, but not the finer sizes of needles.

Milliner's or straw needles, size 9, can also be used. They are long and flexible but have a rounder eye than a beading needle. A sharps size 12 is fine and short. It will work perfectly well if you prefer a shorter needle.

Tip
Test the needle on the beads you are going to use to make sure the needle's eye and the thread will pass easily through the bead. If it is tight, the thread will wear and become weak, so choose the correct size of needle for your work.

Thimble

A thimble is optional. Occasionally you will need to push the needle hard through a bead which is full of thread. A thimble will protect you from damaging the end of your finger.

Velvet or felt pads

It is useful to have a piece of felt or velvet to put your beads on whilst working. The fabric stops the beads from rolling about and getting lost. Felt will do, but fibres from it tend to get woven into the purse. Furnishing velvet works best as it has a short pile and is not hairy like felt. I have made a velvet bag, which I stuffed with sawdust, but a bean bag would also work.

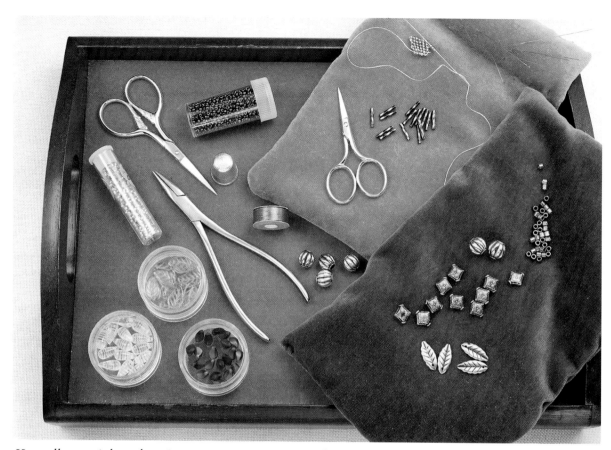

Keep all materials and equipment necessary on a tray for easy access

The bag should be loosely stuffed so that you can make indentations in it to hold the different colours of beads you are working with. A pad approximately 10 x 18cm (4 x 7in) is adequate.

I also have a small tray lined with velvet and I work with a pad, my current thread and scissors in the tray. The beads are contained in the tray so they can be sorted and put away easily. I can move anywhere to work and feel that everything is safely contained.

Scissors

Normal embroidery scissors are all that are required when working beading.

Pliers

A small pair of stainless steel pliers comes in useful for pulling needles through beads that have many threads through them. Care has to be taken not to break the bead, so pull gently holding the bead firmly.

Magnifying glass

A magnifying glass is useful when threading finer needles.

Bead storage

It is essential to have lidded containers to store your beads in. Hexagonal containers, available from fly-fishing suppliers, are extremely good.

13   Sheila Paton
       Jean Milne

20   Christine McLeod
       Hazel Henley

27   Jean Brown
       Anne Hamilton

DECEMBER

4   Christmas tea.

A single lid can be lifted to empty out one type of bead. Unfortunately these boxes are not readily available. The larger boxes which have about 18 different compartments are excellent for storing different shades of beads so that they are easily accessible. I find that a salt spoon is useful for scooping the beads out of their compartments. Circular stacking boxes also work well, providing they are screwed together properly.

Thread

Nymo is a special thread used for beading, and is available from embroidery shops and specialist bead suppliers. I have found that this brand works best. It consists of a long filament which is extremely strong, which is essential when working with beads because a broken thread means beads everywhere.

Nymo comes in different thicknesses: D and B are for general use, O is finer. B is the thread most often used, and can be obtained in a wide range of colours. The type I use is supplied on small reels, like sewing machine spools. When the spool is nearly empty the thread comes off a bit like a corkscrew. It can be easily straightened out by running dampened fingers down it. It can also be dampened and pressed flat with your fingers to make it easier to thread your beading needle.

Nymo does not knot as much as some threads do. This is a big advantage because it means that you can work with a long thread, which saves ending and joining in new threads. When threads end and new threads are introduced, the beads get filled with thread making further work through them difficult. This applies particularly to bugle beads, which are often used for the neck of the purse and

will contain the thread which joins them together to form a neck, as well as the threads joining the body of the purse.

Nymo is available in a large range of colours, including gold. It isn't too important to match the colour of the thread exactly with the beads as almost all of the thread will be inside or between the beads. I would recommend a dark colour for dark beads and a paler colour for light ones. Where mixed colours of beads are used, choose a colour to match the beads you are going to use the most of. It is not practical to keep changing the thread.

Types of beads

Beads come in all shapes, sizes and colours. For the purses in this book, I have used small round beads, Delicas, and bugle beads. For the decorative chains and fringes, any size and shape of bead can be used so long as it suits the purse. The larger the number used to describe the size of the bead, the smaller the bead.

Containers which allow you to see and reach the beads easily are essential

Small round beads, as used in the projects, are supplied in two sizes: the smallest is size 11, size 10 is slightly larger. They are often referred to as seed beads or rocailles and come in a wide range of colours and decorative finishes, including frosted.

A more limited range of colours is available in the larger size 8 beads. All the patterns featured in this book could be worked in size 8 beads, or even size 6, which will result in a bigger purse. These larger sizes are also useful for chains and fringes and for variations in netted and square netted purses.

> *Tip*
> *It is best to work with beads of one size as a slight size difference can show. I have used 10s and 11s together, but make up a sample first to see what effect the difference in size has on the tension and the finished look of the work.*

Hexagonal beads, size 11, look faceted and can be worked into the pattern in the place of small round beads to give a textured appearance to your work.

Delica beads have a large hole in relation to their size and are cylindrical in shape. They come in sizes 11 and 8, and are available in a range of colours. They look lovely and are delightful to use, especially for peyote and square stitch work, but they cost more than round beads. They are available through specialist bead suppliers.

Bugle beads are long narrow beads, often used for the neck of a purse and in chains and fringes. They are sold in different lengths, 6mm (¼in) is a good size to choose, but other lengths are useful, especially for chains and fringes.

Twisted bugles are very attractive and are usually about 8mm or 10mm (about ⅜in) long. Twisted bugle beads work best with round beads while straight bugle beads work best with Delicas.

When you are buying bugle beads, examine them carefully – the ones sold to embroiderers often vary in length. This will show if you are making a neck or fringe, where the beads should look even.

Really long bugle beads, e.g. 15mm, can be used in the fringes and chains, so all sizes are worth collecting.

Large beads have rather large holes so may have to be rejected as they will slip over smaller beads. Graded sizes can help prevent this. Charms can be used and small semi-precious stones are also available in many different colours and sizes with holes drilled for easy threading.

Buying beads

Bearing in mind that the finished size of the average purse is 4 x 5cm (1⅜ x 2in), collect beads – glass, metal or wood – which you think will be suitable. They can be bought from specialist mail-order suppliers or you can use beads from discarded necklaces. Beaded items can often be found in charity shops. New suppliers are entering the market all the time so a greater variety of beads is becoming more readily available.

Beads are often sold pre-packed. This is a useful way of obtaining small amounts, sometimes less than five grams, of a variety of colours which are very useful when you come to do patterned work. Specialist suppliers often pack their beads in tubes which hold 10 grams which are a much better buy. Delicas generally come in five gram tubes.

For background colours, it is better to buy in larger amounts, e.g. 20 gram or 100 gram packs. It is a good idea to club together with a group of people to buy large quantities of beads, which can then be shared out. This saves on postage as well as on the price of the beads and will allow you to build up a good collection of colours. It is difficult to buy exactly the right number of beads for a single project. It is not practical to do so as it is inevitable that some beads will be lost while making the purse.

If you buy the very small, bubble seal, pre-packaged beads, you will find there are 4.54 grams in the glass seed bead packs. Antique beads usually come in 2.63 gram packs.

I have not quoted amounts of less than five grams for making the purses, although sometimes a smaller amount will usually be adequate. Try and estimate the number of beads needed from the chart. It is better to buy more beads than you need to build up stocks of colours.

Always try to buy good quality beads. It is difficult to get any guarantee that the colours will stay fast and not wear off as time goes on. Buying from a specialist supplier should mean that the beads are of a high quality and are from a satisfactory source.

Jewellery findings

Jewellery findings are the fittings, usually of metal, which make a piece of craftwork into a wearable item of jewellery. Pins for brooches, clasps for necklaces and bracelets, hooks, clips or studs for earrings are all examples. Findings are made in various metals – brass, copper and steel. Some are chrome, silver or gold plated. At the top of the scale there are solid gold and silver findings.

Specialist bead merchants stock a range of findings, they can also be found in some craft and embroidery shops but it may be necessary to consult a working jeweller if you wanted findings made in the precious metals.

A selection of jewellery findings

CHAPTER 2

TECHNIQUES

This chapter describes how to work the main stitches used to make the purses. It is worth spending time and materials practising the stitches by making a sample using each stitch. There are a few general points which are widely applicable. When working any of these sample stitches, you may find it easier to use larger beads at first, then work a second sample using size 10 round beads. I used size 8 beads so that the pattern of the stitch shows up clearly in the photographs.

Tension
Stitch tension is important in all forms of needlework, and beaded purses are no exception. Unnecessary gaps between the beads show, especially between bugle beads because they are long and straight, so the eye can easily pick out any discrepancies.

Starting work
When beginning work with round or Delica beads you need to attach the first bead to the thread. Thread the needle and take it through the bead twice, leaving a 10–13cm (4–5⅛in) tail. The double stitch secures the bead and the tail gives you something to hold on to while you are working. Later, you can stitch the tail into the work to finish it off.

Finishing and joining new threads
To finish off a thread within the work, pass the thread through the work you have done, following the pattern of the beads as far as possible. See the diagram with each individual stitch instruction.

To begin a new thread, follow the same pattern as for finishing the thread, making sure you bring out the thread where you need it.

The neck

I often use bugle beads for the neck of the purse; they give a smart edge to the work and the difference in texture adds interest.

Tip
Do not use any damaged bugle beads as their chipped edges are very sharp. They will eventually cut the thread and spoil your purse.

MATERIALS AND EQUIPMENT

20 bugle beads
Beading needle, size 10
Nymo thread
Velvet pad or piece of felt
Embroidery scissors

1

Count out 10 bugle beads onto your velvet pad or tray and put the rest back in their container. Examine the beads carefully. Dispose of any damaged beads and replace them immediately so you will be sure that you have 10 beads on the neck when you are working.

Tip

Tension is important when you are adding the bugle beads. Do not pull the beads together too tightly, but try to keep the tension of the thread even so that the beads are only just touching one another.

2

Thread the beading needle with 1m (about 3¼ft) of Nymo. Pick up two bugle beads and thread them onto the needle. Pull the beads to the end of the thread leaving approximately 13cm (5⅛in) as a tail.

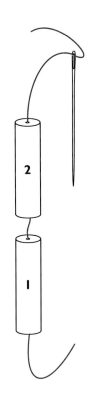

3

Fold the thread so that bugle beads 1 and 2 lie side by side. Take the needle up through bugle bead 1, the one with the 13cm (5⅛in) tail hanging from it. Pull the needle through, then take it down through bugle bead 2 again. Repeat this process by going up through bead 1 and down bead 2 to secure the two beads.

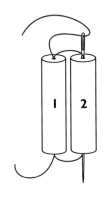

4

Add the rest of the bugle beads as follows. Pick up bugle bead 3 with the needle and pull it onto the thread. Take the needle down through bugle bead 2 and pull the thread up so that bugle bead 3 lies alongside bugle bead 2. Take the needle up through bead 3.

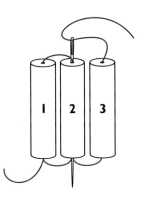

Add bugle bead 4, then take the needle up through bugle bead 3.

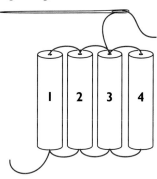

You will not be able to add the next bead until you have worked the needle down through bead 4. You can now add bugle bead 5 and continue until all 10 bugle beads needed have been added.

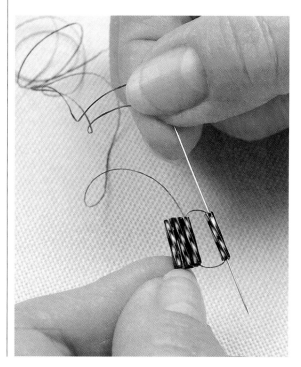

When all 10 beads are connected, work the thread through beads 9 and 10 again. You should then have a length of thread left in the needle which is hanging from bugle bead 10.

Tip
When making a purse it is useful to have some thread left after working the neck; you can then begin the purse without immediately having to join in another thread.

Using round beads

Bugle beads are not available in the same range of colours as round beads. If the colour of the neck of the purse is critical you can use three or five round beads instead of one bugle bead, working them in the same way as above.

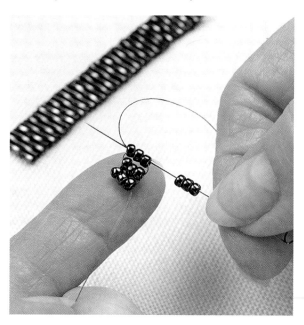

Joining a thread

If it is necessary to join up a thread when stitching the bugle beads, work as follows. Take the needle with the new thread up through the bugle bead four back from where the thread ran out, leave a tail of thread hanging out of the bead.

Work down through the third bead, back up through the fourth bead, down through the third bead, up through the second bead and down through the bead where the thread ran out. The thread is now in the correct position to continue.

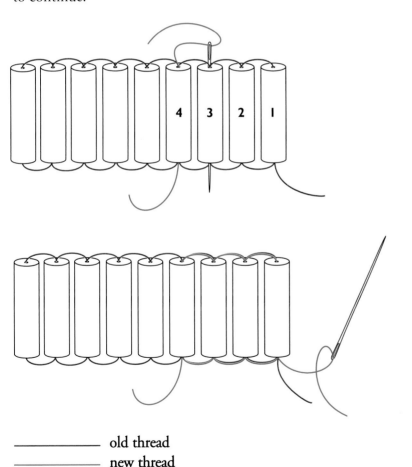

_____ old thread
_____ new thread

Brick stitch

Beads worked in brick stitch follow the same pattern as bricks in a wall. The beads are not attached directly underneath one another, but are moved along so that each row of beads is offset by half a bead.

The beads hang on the threads which join together the beads in the row above. This means that row 1 must be joined so that there is a thread between each bead. Begin your sample by joining the first row of round beads in the same way as the bugle beads for the neck of a purse. The beads are small, so this may prove fiddly until you are used to handling them. Persevere as practice does help. You can use size 8 beads to begin with then try another sample with one of the smaller sizes.

MATERIALS AND EQUIPMENT
5 grams round beads, size 11, 10 or 8
Beading needle, size 10
Nymo thread
Velvet or felt pad
Embroidery scissors

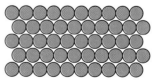

Brick stitch – beads arranged like bricks in a wall

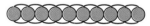

The beads are joined so that there is a thread between each bead

STEP
1

Thread a beading
needle with 1.5m
(5ft) of thread.
Count out 10 round
beads onto the
velvet pad. Pick up
one bead and work
through it twice.

STEP
2

Pull the bead to the
end of the thread
leaving a tail about
13cm (5⅛in) long.
Pick up another
bead and thread it
onto the needle.
Fold the thread so
that beads 1 and 2
lie side by side.

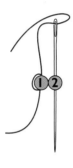

STEP
3

Take the needle up
through bead 1. Pull
the needle through,
then take it down
through bead 2 again.
Repeat this process
by going up through
bead 1 and down
through bead 2 to
secure the two beads
so that they stay in
position whilst you
continue the work.

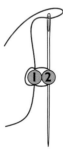

STEP
4

Add the rest of the beads as follows. Pick up
bead 3 with the needle and pull it onto the
thread. Take the needle down through bead 2
and pull the thread up so that bead 3 lies
alongside bead 2. You will see that the thread
is coming from bead 2 and it is impossible to
add another bead satisfactorily to lie next to
bead 3. You must therefore take the needle up
through bead 3.

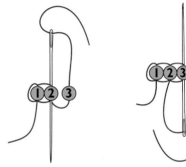

STEP
5

Add bead 4, then take the needle up through
bead 3. Again you will not be able to add the
next bead until you have worked the needle
down through bead 4. You can now add bead 5
and continue until all 10 beads have been added.

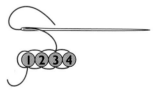

Step

6

After connecting the 10 beads, carefully count out another 10 beads of the same size ready for the second row. Holding the work in your left hand, and the needle in your right hand (work the opposite way if you are left handed), pick up two beads. Take the needle under the thread joining beads 10 and 9. Pull the thread through so that the beads are pulled up close to the first row.

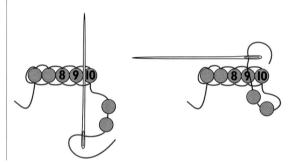

Step

7

At this point the beads appear to be lying with their holes parallel to the first row. Take the needle over the joining thread and back through the first of the two beads making sure that the needle goes into the bead at the same end as it last came out.

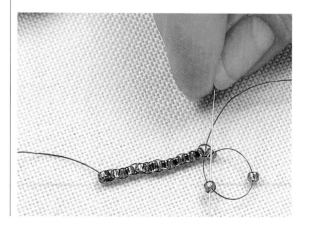

Step

8

Pull the new beads up to the first row. This action not only attaches the beads to the first row, but also turns the beads on their sides so that the thread is in place ready to add the next bead. Pick up one bead on the needle and take the needle under the thread joining beads 8 and 9 in first row. Take the needle over the connecting thread and back through the bead.

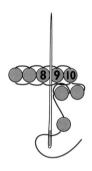

Step

9

Continue adding beads in this way until 10 beads are attached. You are now at the point where you can pick up another two beads and begin a third row, working from left to right. If you find it difficult to reverse the order of work, turn the work over to its other side and work from right to left.

10

Add two beads at the beginning of each row, then add one bead at a time to complete the row. If the sample was joined to make a circle you would find 10 connecting threads, so you would need to add one bead at a time. As the work is flat you only have nine connecting threads between the beads, so you need to add two beads at the beginning of each row in order to maintain 10 beads per row.

Tip
Take the needle diagonally through the beads to hide any spare thread. This is useful for ending and beginning threads. Threads taken across from one bead to the next will, to some extent, also disappear between the beads, but it is best to work diagonally where possible.

11

To finish off the sample, work through the beads diagonally and across to the next bead. Continue around twice then run the thread through the beads away from the diamond. Cut off the thread close to the beads. Work the tail left at the beginning into the sample in the same way.

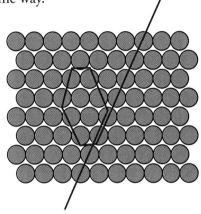

Square stitch

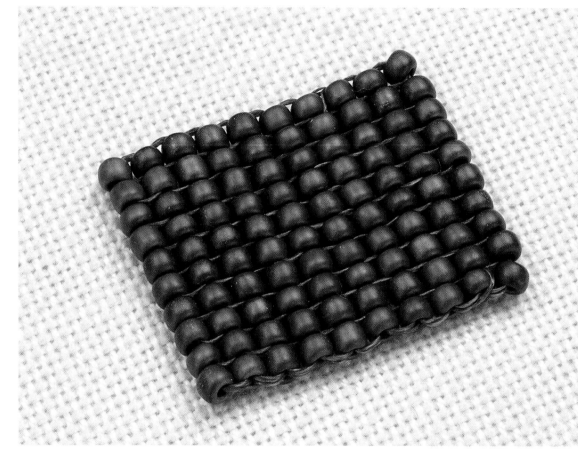

Square stitch is a versatile stitch which allows you to work patterns with straight lines as well as diagonal ones.

MATERIALS AND EQUIPMENT
5 grams round beads, size 10 or 8
Beading needle, size 10
Nymo thread
Velvet pad or piece of felt
Embroidery scissors

STEP

1

Thread a beading needle with 1.5m (about 5ft) of Nymo. Pick up one bead on the needle. Leave a 13cm (5⅛in) tail then work the needle twice through the bead.

STEP

2

Pick up another nine beads with the needle and pull the thread through them. You should now have 10 beads on a straight thread. This is the full width of the sample.

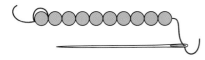

STEP

3

Pick up another bead and take the needle through the tenth bead of the first row from left to right. Take the needle through the first bead of the second row from right to left.

STEP

4

You are now ready to pick up the next bead of the second row and work through bead 9 of the first row. Continue across in this way to complete the row.

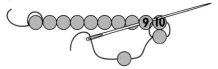

STEP

5

When you reach the end of the second row, bead 10 should be beneath bead 1 of the first row. The thread should come out of bead 10 of the second row. Take the needle from left to right through the beads of the first row.

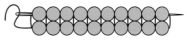

STEP

6

Take the needle all the way back through the second row, from right to left. This strengthens the work and makes all the beads in a row line up.

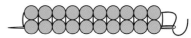

STEP

7

Pick up another bead and repeat the process as above. This time you will be working from left to right. Work 10 rows.

STEP

8

To finish off, work the thread back into the sample in squares.

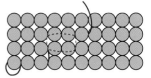

Peyote stitch

To work a sample of peyote stitch it will be helpful to use beads in two contrasting colours and use a larger size of bead (I used size 8). I find it easier to teach this stitch using very large red and green beads.

The larger beads and the two colours will help you to see how the rows are formed. Once you have mastered peyote stitch you will find it quick and easy.

Tip

It is important to realize from the beginning that you are working up and down the sample, not across as for brick stitch. The two colours make alternate rows.

MATERIALS AND EQUIPMENT

5 grams round beads of two colours (light and dark), size 8
Beading needle, size 10
Nymo thread
Velvet pad or piece of felt
Embroidery scissors

STEP 1

Thread the needle with 1.5m (about 5ft) of Nymo. Count out 10 light and 10 dark beads.

Tip

An even number of each is needed for the following instructions. If you use an odd number of beads the ends of the rows should be worked differently.

STEP 2

Pick up one dark bead and work through it twice. Alternating the colours, thread a further 19 beads onto the Nymo. Pick up a bead the same colour as light bead 20 and take the needle through the dark bead 19 from right to left.

STEP 3

Pick up another light bead and take the needle through dark bead 17, from right to left. Continue across, picking up only light beads and working the needle through only the dark beads. At this stage it is not easy to maintain the correct tension, but persevere. Pull the thread up firmly at the end of each row. It gets easier as you progress.

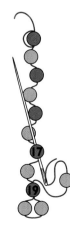

STEP 4

For the next row, pick up a dark bead and pass the needle through the first light bead. Continue the row, picking up only dark beads and work the needle through only light beads.

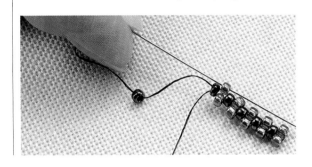

STEP 5

Continue in this way, alternating the colours. This will result in a striped sample.

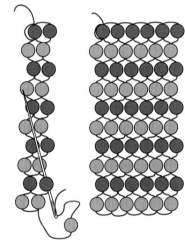

STEP 6

Add a thread by working into the beads, as shown by the black line. Finish off by working into the beads in the same way.

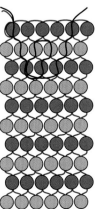

Netting

Netting makes a very attractive purse. The stitch is easy to work and produces a purse quickly.

In five-bead netting you need to add beads in multiples of six. The five in five-bead netting refers to the number of beads between the common beads in the net. In this case the common bead is the sixth bead.

If you were making a three-bead net you would pick up multiples of four. That way you see three beads forming a net between the common fourth bead.

Five-bead net

Three-bead net

MATERIALS AND EQUIPMENT

5 grams round beads, size 10 or 8, in each of three colours (my sample is worked in purple, apricot and orange)
Beading needle, size 10
Nymo thread
Velvet pad or piece of felt
Embroidery scissors

STEP
1

Starting with a purple bead, work through it twice to secure the bead onto the thread. Pick up another 23 beads, keeping to the following colour combination: 1 purple (this one is already on the thread), 2 orange, 1 apricot, 2 orange.

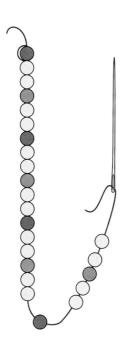

STEP
2

Once you have 24 beads on your thread pull them up close to one another. Count back 12 beads to the thirteenth bead from the top, a purple bead in the sample. Take the needle through this bead and pull the thread gently through so that the beads form a loop.

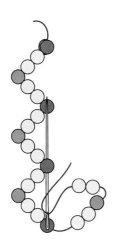

STEP
3

Pick up five beads, keeping the colours in the correct order: 2 orange, 1 apricot, 2 orange. Take the needle through the seventh bead from the top, pull the thread through so that the five beads you have added form another loop.

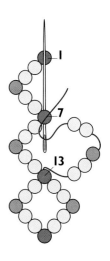

STEP
4

Add another five beads and take the needle through bead 1. Pick up eight beads in the following order: 2 orange, 1 apricot, 2 orange, 1 purple, 2 orange. Take the needle through the bead marked X in the diagram, an apricot bead.

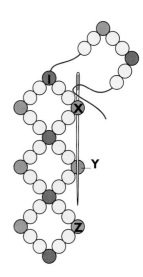

STEP
5

Add another five beads – 2 orange, 1 purple, 2 orange – and work through the next apricot bead marked Y. Add another five beads and work through the bead marked Z. You will see that you have added five beads in the same order, always going through an apricot bead.

Tip
To improve the tension, pull the thread up tight whilst holding the top or bottom bead at the opposite end of the row to the needle.

STEP
6

Add eight beads in the correct order to form the bottom diamond net. Adding five beads in the correct order and, working through the purple bead each time, work to the top of the row.

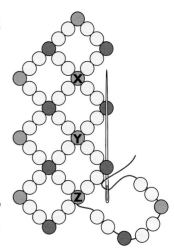

STEP
7

You should now be able to see that the colour of bead you work through in one row is constant and that the colour alternates with each row. So, if you are working through a purple bead, the central bead of the five you pick up is apricot. The purple and apricot beads form rows across the sample, making it easy to see that your work is correct.

STEP
8

Continue working in this way until you have eight diamonds across the bottom. Finish off the thread by working through the beads.

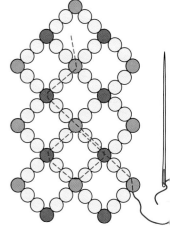

Tip

To see the shape of the netting, run spare needles through the top and
bottom beads of the sample. This is particularly helpful when you are
using size 8 beads, as the holes in the beads are rather large for the thread.

Square netting

Square netting consists of a series of circles of beads joined together by circles of thread. Because the beads form circles, a diamond-shaped hole will appear where four circles come together. The thread should not go across these holes, as they form an integral part of the pattern. You have to work round the circle, without crossing the hole, in order to get to a point where you can add more beads.

This net is often called right-angled weave because the thread does a right-angle turn at each corner of the circle or square. The size of the square obviously depends on the number of beads you put on each side. For the sample, I have made a mesh of three beads per side.

MATERIALS AND EQUIPMENT

5 grams round beads, size 10
50 beads, size 8
Beading needle, size 10
Nymo thread
Velvet pad or piece of felt
Embroidery scissors

Removing extra beads

If you have added an extra bead to the mesh, and the mistake is too far back to undo, break the bead by squeezing it gently with a small pair of snipe-nosed pliers. The tension may be loose, but the number of beads will be correct.

If you have missed off a bead, you must undo the work and start again.

TEP

1

Pick up 12 beads on the thread, leaving a 13cm (5⅛in) tail. Work the needle through all 12 beads again to form a loose circle and through the first nine beads once more, to secure the thread.

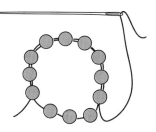

TEP

2

Hold the circle of beads in your left hand with the tail on the left and the needle thread coming from the right of the circle. Pick up nine beads. Take the needle down through three beads, labelled 7, 8 and 9 in the diagram.

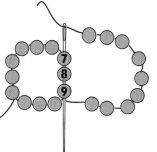

TEP

3

Work the needle through the first six beads you have just added.

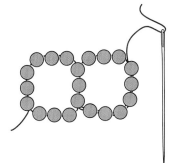

Tip

When you are working back through the beads, work through three beads at a time, not six. This helps ensure good tension and ensures the correct number of beads are added. Great care is needed to keep the numbers accurate.

STEP

4

Pick up nine beads. Take the needle up through three beads of the previous square. As before, take the needle through the first six beads just added. You will find that you are making a series of circles rather than squares.

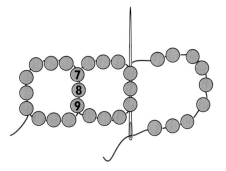

STEP

5

When you have done three or four circles lay the work down flat and push them into squares. This will help you see if the circles will form squares. More thread is needed for a square. If the thread is too tight the squares will not form. To rectify this, ease the thread back through the squares.

STEP
6

Continue working across the row, the arrows show the direction in which the needle should be pointing when you join up the previous squares. Work a row of 10 squares. To complete the tenth square, work through three beads, not six, so that you are in the correct position to start the row below.

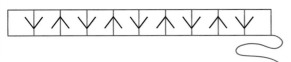

STEP
7

Pick up 9 beads and work through the three beads at the base of the tenth square.

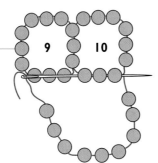

STEP
8

Work round the square, through the nine beads you have just added. Turn and run the thread through three beads of square 9.

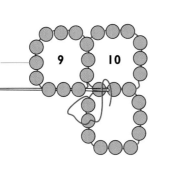

STEP
9

At this point you will see that you already have two sides of the next square in position. Pick up six beads.

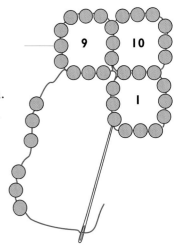

STEP
10

Continue working across to complete the second row. The arrows in the diagram show the direction you should be working in. The small red lines indicate the points at which you can leave the circles.

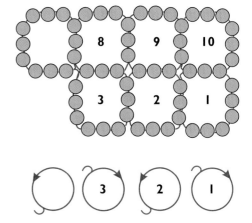

11

Square 10 of the second row should be under square 1 of the first row. After completing square 10, the thread has to emerge from the right-hand base. Pick up nine beads and complete square 1 of the third row.

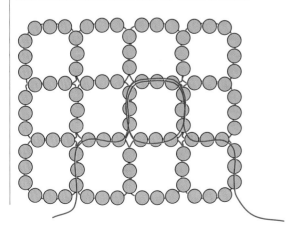

12

Continue working in this way until you have five rows of 10 squares.

13

To finish off, or begin a new thread, work several times round a circle and then through the mesh. Take care not to cross a hole.

14

Secure a new thread, or use what is left from making the mesh. Bring the thread out at point A in the diagram. Pick up one size 8 bead. Take the needle diagonally across the square and thread it from left to right through the three small beads of the square.

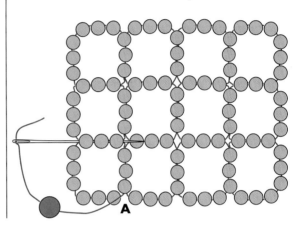

15

Pull the thread up gently so that the large bead lies in the centre of the square. Continue in this way, filling the squares. Follow the thread lines in the diagram to complete the filling of the mesh. The diagonal thread lines form a zigzag pattern across the mesh.

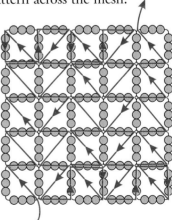

Chapter 3

DECORATIVE FINISHES

The purses require a decorative finish of some sort at the base and sometimes at the neck. They will also need chains if you are to wear them, or wish to hang them up as decorative features in your home.

Chains

When selecting beads for the chain try to choose beads which will complement those used in the purse. Larger, colourful beads can add interest, but don't be tempted to detract from the purse by making the chain too elaborate. I often leave the middle third of the chain very plain. This saves using expensive decorative beads, and makes the purse more comfortable to wear.

If you are adding beads with large holes you will have to look carefully at the beads either side. They may disappear into the large bead if they are smaller than the hole, making the chain look uneven.

I have given a chain plan with each purse pattern, but you may wish to work to your own designs. Make sure you attach chains securely or you will risk losing the purse and even some valuable beads. Two threads used separately add strength; should one break or come loose the other thread will keep the chain intact.

Attaching a chain

Step
1

Thread the needle with 1.5m (about 5ft) of Nymo and work it into the purse securely. Bring the needle out at one side of the purse through the neck beads. Thread the beads to make a chain about 65cm (26in) long. Pull the thread up firmly and make sure there are no gaps between the purse and the beads or between the beads of the chain.

Step
2

Secure the thread by working through the neck beads into the purse beads. Take a second 1.5m (about 5ft) length of thread. Attach it securely and thread it through the chain beads. Secure at the other end.

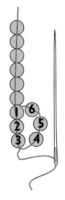

Loops

While making the chain you can create loops of beads by threading on five or six small beads and working through them again. They look more attractive if you work through beads 1 and 2 again, or even through bead 3. This makes a loop to one side of the chain.

Circles

To make a circle, work with two needles at the same time. Attach both threads at the beginning

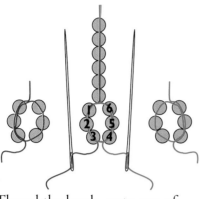

of the chain. Thread the beads, onto one of the threads, where you want a circle. Using one thread, work through the six beads clockwise then through beads 1, 2 and 3. Using the second thread work through the six beads anticlockwise then through beads 6, 5 and 4. The two needles should come out at the same point so you are ready to add the next bead of the chain on both threads.

Tip

Keep the two needles at the same point. If you work with one needle first, then try to put through the second one you will find that the tension from the first thread is too tight to pull into well-formed circles.

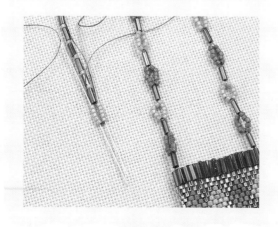

Bugle beads

You can use bugle beads decoratively by threading and securing the chain on one thread, then taking the second needle through the chain to the point where you want to add more bugle beads. To add a bugle, or even two or three small beads to the central first bugle, follow the diagrams.

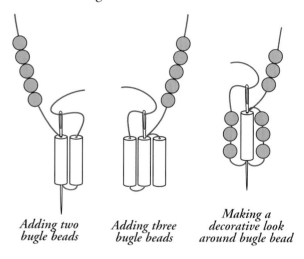

Adding two bugle beads   *Adding three bugle beads*   *Making a decorative look around bugle bead*

Twisted chains

Attach two threads, both at one side of the purse. Fill each thread with beads, making them even in length. Twist the two lengths of beads together and then attach both threads to the opposite side of the purse without letting the twist go.

Repetitive patterns

When threading a chain with a repetitive pattern you may have to reverse the pattern when you reach the centre of the chain. If you don't do this you will find that you have an opposite pattern at each side of the purse. To correct this, thread on half the beads then reverse the pattern.

Netted chains

A beautiful chain can be made using the netting method. I worked my chain using a three-bead net (see page 22). I think that this is wide enough for the chain of a decorative purse. If you are going to make larger purses than the ones featured in this book then a five-bead net would work better.

This type of chain can also be used as a spectacles chain with the appropriate findings stitched to the ends. A shorter length could also make a lovely choker by attaching a jewellery fastener to the ends.

MATERIALS AND EQUIPMENT

10 grams each of two colours of small round beads, I used silver (A) and black (B)
Reel of Nymoe thread
Size 10 beading needle

STEP
1

Secure a bead, colour A, leaving a tail. Add five beads in the following order, 1B, 1A, 2B, 1A (for a five-bead net the pattern runs: 2B, 1A, 3B, 1A). Turn and work back through the second bead back (the first B). The first bead acts as a stop bead.

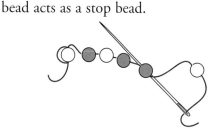

Tip
Hold the tail thread in your left hand and the stop bead between the first two fingers of your right hand. Tighten the thread with the little finger and thumb of your right hand.

STEP
2

Add three beads (1B, 1A, 1B). Work through the first bead you picked up, the one with the tail hanging from it.

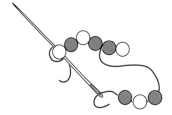

Bead Key
A = silver   B = black

STEP
3

Pick up 2B, 1A. Turn back and work through the middle bead you have just added.

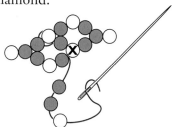

STEP
4

Add three beads (1B, 1A, 1B) and work through the bead marked X, at the bottom of the first diamond.

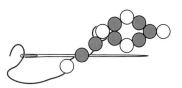

STEP
5

Pick up another three beads (2B, 1A). Turn back and work through the first B bead you have just added. Add three more beads (1B, 1A, 1B). Work through the bead labelled Y.

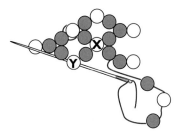

STEP
6

Add three beads (2B, 1A) and work back through the first B bead.

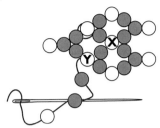

STEP
7

Add (1B, 1A, 1B) and work through the bead labelled Z. You can now see a pattern emerging. This is continued by adding three beads (2B, 1A), working back through the first B bead then adding another three beads (1B, 1A, 1B) to complete the off-centre diamond between each side.

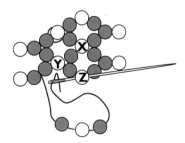

Decorative tops

A decorative top can be added to a plain
beaded purse or one with bugles at the neck.

Looped top

STEP
1

To make a looped top, bring a thread out of a neck bead. Thread on five or seven small round beads. Take the needle down through the next but one neck bead. Bring the needle up through the empty neck bead between the two neck beads you have just used.

STEP
2

Thread another five or seven small beads and take the needle down through the next but one neck bead. Continue round the top of the purse, finishing off the thread securely where you started.

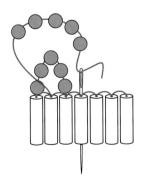

Looped top variations

This top can only be used if the total number of beads in the neck is divisible by three.

STEP
1

Attach a thread and bring it out through a neck bead. Thread on five or seven small beads and take the needle down through the next but one neck bead.

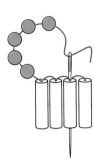

STEP
2

Bring the needle up through the next neck bead and repeat the process round the purse.

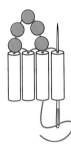

STEP
3

If the number of beads in the neck is not divisible by three, but can be divided by two then each neck bead can be used.

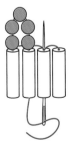

Tip
Try varying the colours of the beads. Interesting effects can also be obtained by using one or more larger beads combined with smaller beads.

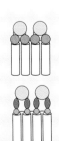

Turret top

STEP
1

Attach a thread and bring it out through a neck bead. Thread on three beads. They can be the same colour. or two colours, bead 2 being a different colour from 1 and 3. Take the needle through the first connecting thread at the top of the neck.

STEP
2

Take the needle back up through the third bead. Thread on two more beads of the correct colour and take the needle through the next connecting thread.

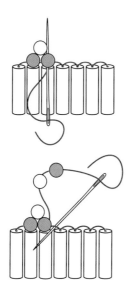

STEP
3

Repeat this process round the top of the purse. When you meet up with the beginning add one bead of the correct colour as shown. Finish off the thread by working it down into the purse.

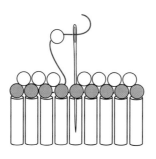

Wavy turret

This is a variation on the turret top. An extra line of beads is added to a turret top and because there is not really enough room for a bead between the turrets it pushes out, creating an attractive wavy edge.

STEP
1

Attach a thread and bring the needle out through the top of the turret you have already added. Thread on one bead then take the needle through the next turret top.

STEP
2

Add another bead and go through the next turret top bead. Continue round the top, finishing off securely.

Fringes

I often make purses with plain backs, so it is only necessary to add a fringe to the front. A fringe on one side is also enough if you have the same pattern on both sides of the purse. If you have a different pattern on both sides of the purse it is worth attaching two fringes, perhaps shorter on one side than the other.

With the charts for the purses you will find charts for the fringes, but there is no reason why you can't design your own fringe. Once you begin to work fringes and chains you will find that the permutations are endless. Try using decorative beads to add interest as I have done on the purse pictured above.

The size and shape of the fringe

Before you start on a fringe, count the number of beads at the base of the purse and decide how many will carry the fringe. When the purse is made up the body of the purse is folded in half. If the body of the purse is 40 beads across, each side will be 20 beads. The fringe should therefore hang on 20 beads. However you might have folded the purse so that you have 19 on each side and one at each end, in which case the fringe would hang on either 19 or 21 beads. You can also decide if you can use the centre bead or leave it blank.

When you have made these choices, decide on the shape of the fringe: straight, pointed or sloping. Then select the beads you want to use. You can work the fringe outwards from the centre or inward from the sides. I usually work from the outside edges, keeping the fringe even.

To attach a fringe

STEP

1

Secure a thread at the base of the purse and bring the needle out through the left-hand bottom bead. Thread on the beads for the fringe. Take the needle back through all the beads you have attached except the last one added. This last bead acts as a stop bead, preventing the thread from slipping back through the beads.

2

Take the
needle up
through the
bottom left
hand bead of
the purse and
down through
the next
bottom bead.

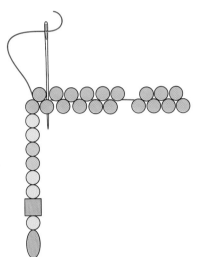

Tip
Check that the thread in the first row of
fringe is pulled up firmly so that there are
no gaps between the beads or between the
fringe and the purse. Tension is important:
too tight and the fringe does not hang
nicely; too loose and the thread shows.

Stop bead variations
The stop bead can also be a few small beads
formed into a loop.

3

Continue adding lines of fringe beads until
the fringe is complete. Secure the thread. If
you need to add a new thread, do this in the
body of the purse and work the thread to
where it is needed.

Decorative beads

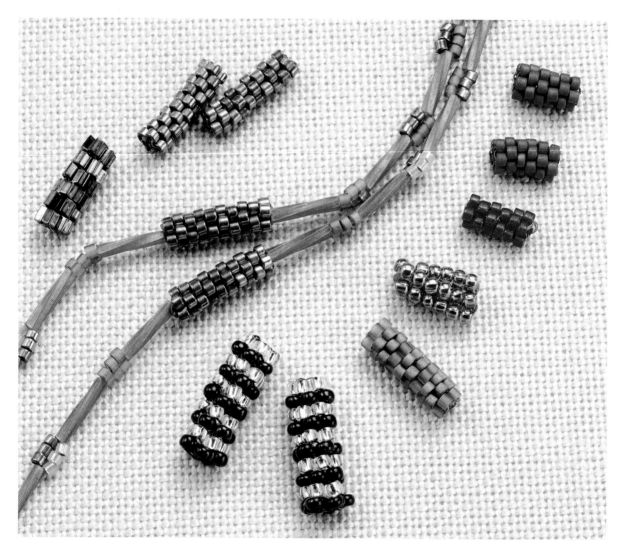

When you are designing chains and fringes, it is not always easy to find decorative beads which match or complement the colours of your purse. You can use peyote, brick stitch and square stitch techniques to make decorative beads from a number of the small beads. These decorative beads will match the purse perfectly and, when added to chains and fringes, make the finished result look professional. They also add texture and dimension.

Peyote-style beads

The length of the bead produced depends on the number of beads you thread when you begin. The more rows you work before joining the complete bead up, the larger the diameter of the finished bead. The hole through the centre will also be larger.

MATERIALS AND EQUIPMENT

Small beads, round or Delicas, very small quantities are needed, a six-bead peyote-style bead uses 24 beads
Nymo thread
Size 10 beading needle

STEP
1

Secure the first of six beads onto the thread. Pick up the remaining five beads. Work two rows of peyote stitch (see page 20).

STEP
2

Work seven or nine rows of peyote. Join the flat peyote into a tight circle. Secure the working thread firmly into the beads. Thread the tail into the needle and secure it into the beads. The peyote bead can now be used in your fringe or chain.

Square-stitch-style beads

MATERIALS AND EQUIPMENT

Small beads, only a small number are needed for each decorative bead, 20 in this example
Nymo thread
Size 10 beading needle

Secure the first of five beads onto the thread. Pick up the other four beads. Work five rows of square stitch (see page 18). Join the work into a circle and secure the end of the thread into the bead. Secure the tail in the bead.

Brick-stitch-style beads

MATERIALS AND EQUIPMENT

Small beads, only a small number are needed for each decorative bead
Nymo thread
Size 10 beading needle

Work five beads across as for a neck. Work five rows of brick stitch (see page 14), adding two beads at the beginning of each row to keep the number of beads per row the same. Join the work into a circle and secure the end of the thread into the bead. Secure the tail in the bead.

Chapter 4

Brick Stitch Purses

The patterns included in this chapter are
some of the designs which I have worked
successfully in brick stitch. The stepped effect
of brick stitch lends itself easily to shapes like
diamonds and triangles.

I find that the most elegant purses are those
where the colour combinations are very
subtle, for instance the Midnight Blues purse
and the Peacock Tail purse. The closer the
colours are to one another the more difficult it
becomes to differentiate between the shades
when you are working, especially under
artificial light. Nevertheless, the end product
is well worth the effort.

The Celtic black purse has been very much
admired for its dramatic design. It is not
possible to create perfect circles in brick stitch,
but the overall pattern is striking.

Purple diamond purse

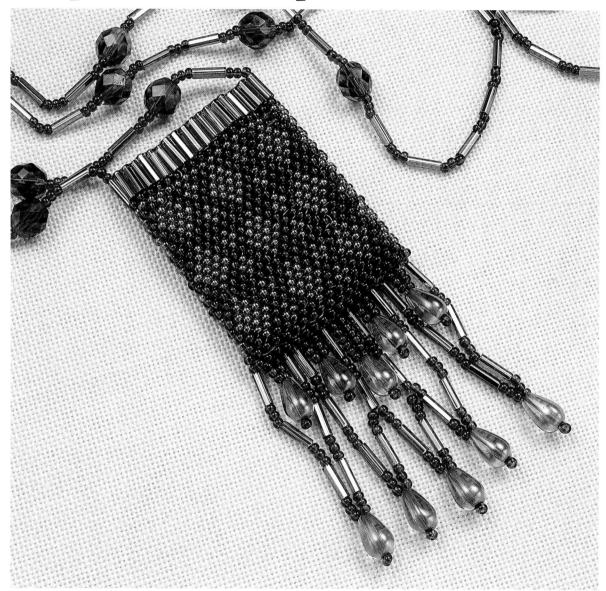

MATERIALS AND EQUIPMENT

Weight of purse: 30 grams
Bugles, iridescent purple (5 grams)
Round beads, pink (10 grams) and
purple (10 grams)

10 large drop beads, iridescent purple
12 large round beads, iridescent purple
Reel of Nymo thread
Size 10 beading needle

Attach chain

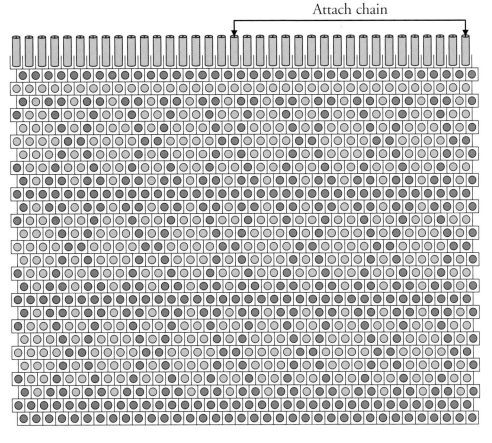

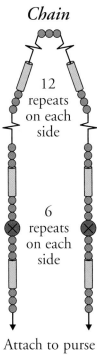

Chain

12
repeats
on each
side

6
repeats
on each
side

Attach to purse

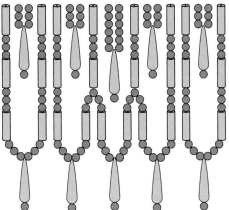

	Bugle, iridescent purple
●	Purple round bead
○	Pink round bead
	Large droplet beads, iridescent purple
⊗	Large round beads, iridescent purple

STEP

1

Place 36 bugles beads on your velvet pad. Examine them for faults. Discard any damaged beads and replace them with good ones.

STEP

2

Make the neck of the purse as instructed in Chapter 2, page 10. When all 36 bugle beads are connected, join them into a circle. Take the needle through bead 1 and through bead 36 and pulling it up close to bead 36. Take the thread through beads 1 and 36 twice more.

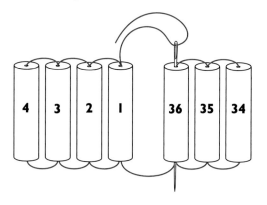

STEP

3

Work the thread through bugle beads 35 and 34 again, bringing the thread out ready to begin adding the round beads in brick stitch.

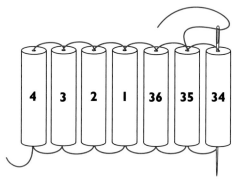

STEP

4

Count out 36 purple round beads onto your velvet pad. Follow the instructions for brick stitch on page 14. Add only one bead at the beginning of each row. This is because you have joined the neck into a circle, you should have 36 joining threads between the bugles. Continue working into the threads at the base of the bugles until all 36 beads have been added.

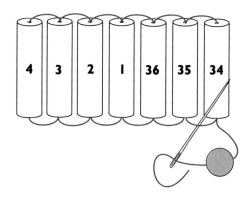

STEP

5

To join the row up and move the thread into position to start the next row, take the needle up through bead 1 and down through bead 2 of the row you have just finished. This brings you to the point where you can begin the second row. You must repeat this process at the end of each row, otherwise you will find yourself working in a spiral and the bottom of the purse will have one side longer than the other.

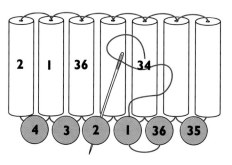

Tip
If you discard any beads during the
work, replace them at once so that you
use the correct number. It will not be
possible to work the chart with an
incorrect number of beads as the repeat
pattern will not work.

Adding the turret top

The method of adding the decorative turret top to the bugle beads is described on page 38. Add the turret top so that the pink is next to the bugle beads: pick up 1 pink, 1 purple, 1 pink bead for the first turret. Then pick up 1 purple, 1 pink bead for the rest of the row, finally adding 1 purple bead.

STEP
6

Add another row of 36 pink beads. Remember to work through two beads before starting the next row. You are now ready to start the pattern following the chart.

STEP
7

Following the chart: pick up a purple bead and attach it to the row above, pick up and attach a pink bead. Work in two more purple beads then a pink bead. Continue the row, repeating two purple and one pink bead until the row is completed with a single purple bead. Then work down to the next row.

Tip
It is best to add a decorative top while
the purse is still open at the bottom.
You can hold the purse by placing two
fingers inside, from the bottom, turning
the purse round as you work.

STEP
8

Continue working the rows of the pattern until you have worked 25 rows, then work two rows of plain purple to finish the purse.

Joining the purse

Fold the purse so that the pattern is even.
The bugle beads can be folded so that there
are 18 on each side or 17 on each side and one
at each end. Use Nymo thread to join up the
bottom of the purse by overcasting the joining
stitches between the beads.

I prefer to join the purse before adding the
fringe; if it is added first it gets in the way
when joining up.

The fringe

Check what beads are required on the chart. You need to add the fringe through the beads of the bottom row of the purse. Take the needle down through the first bead. Pick up all the beads for the first line of the fringe, plus one small bead to act as a stop, see page 40. Take the needle round the small bead then go back through the drop-shaped bead and add the rest of the beads. Go back up through the fourth bead along, at the base of the purse, and down through the next bead. You are now ready to add the beads for the rest of the fringe.

The chain

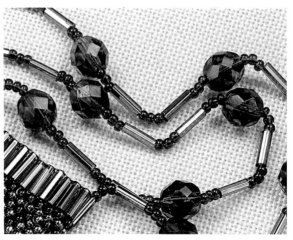

Thread the needle with 1.5m (about 5ft) of Nymo. Work it through the purse, bringing it out at the side of the purse. Thread on the beads in the order shown on the chart, or to your own design. When you have sufficient beads for the length of chain you require finish off the thread very securely in the purse. Connect the second thread and go through the chain in the opposite direction.

Tip
Complete the long elements of the fringe first, then add the beads for the shorter fringe.

Tip
When adding the neck chain the most important point is to make it secure. There is no point in spending time making the purse only to lose it as soon as you wear it.

Turquoise diamond purse

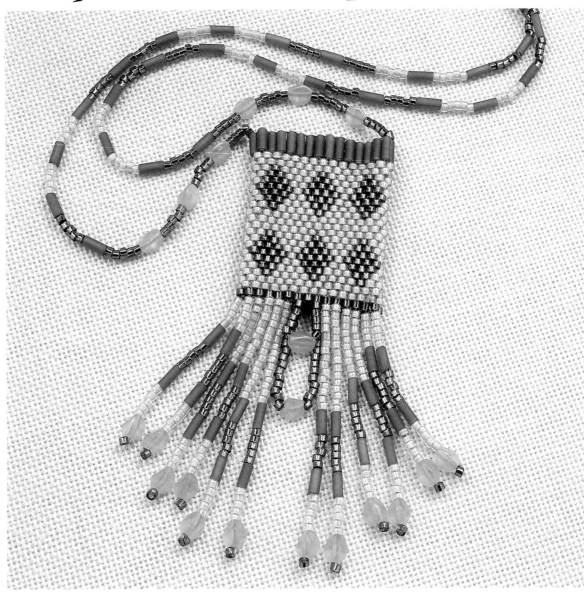

MATERIALS AND EQUIPMENT

Weight of purse: 10 grams
Round beads, dark turquoise (5 grams), pale
turquoise (5 grams)
Bugles, dull turquoise (5 grams)

20 decorative pale blue beads
Reel of Nymo
Size 10 beading needle

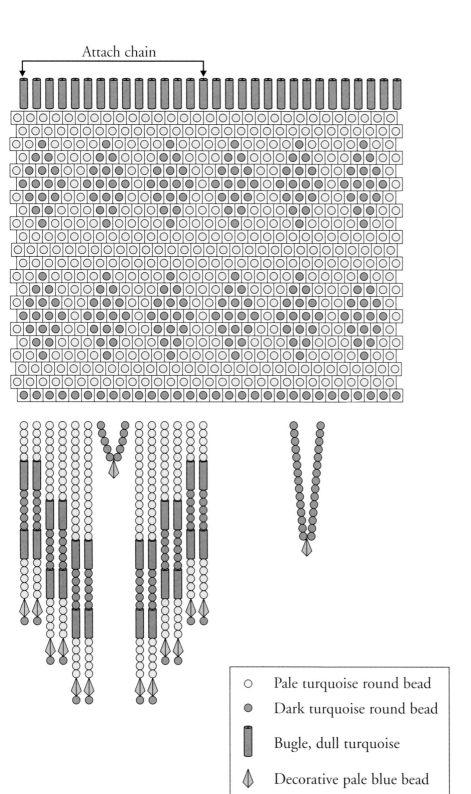

Attach chain

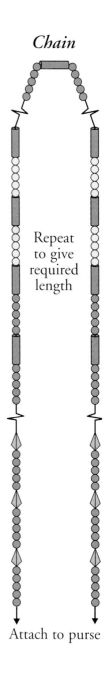

Chain

Repeat
to give
required
length

Attach to purse

○   Pale turquoise round bead

●   Dark turquoise round bead

▮   Bugle, dull turquoise

◈   Decorative pale blue bead

Midnight blues purse

MATERIALS AND EQUIPMENT

Weight of purse: 15 grams
Round beads, blue grey (10 grams), dark blue
(5 grams) and iridescent blue (5 grams)

Bugles, iridescent blue (5 grams)
Reel of Nymo
Size 10 beading needle

Attach chain

Add turret top when
purse is complete

Chain

Repeat
to give
required
length

Attach to purse

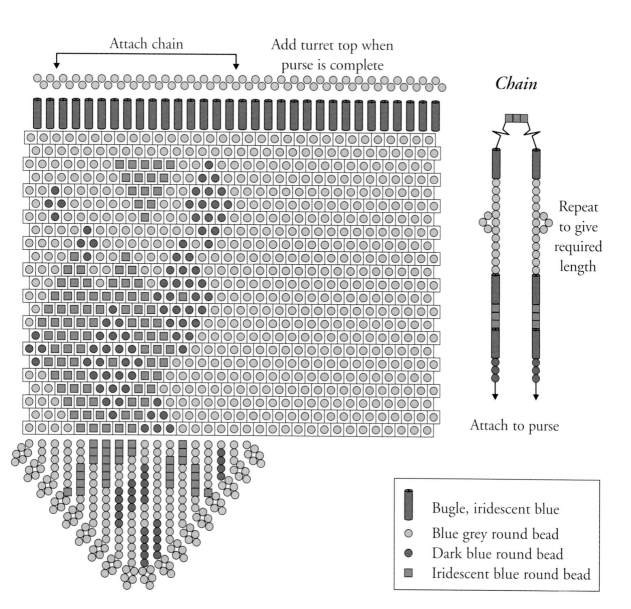

	Bugle, iridescent blue
	Blue grey round bead
	Dark blue round bead
	Iridescent blue round bead

Diamond stripe purse

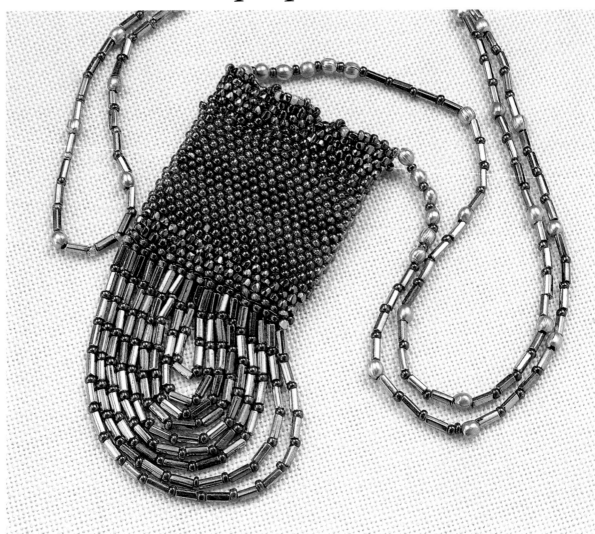

MATERIALS AND EQUIPMENT

Weight of purse: 25 grams
Round beads, gold (5 grams),
red (5 grams), iridescent green (5 grams),
iridescent pink (5 grams)

Bugles, gold (10 grams)
37 large round decorative beads, gold
Reel of Nymo
Size 10 beading needle

Attach chain

Add wavy turret top when
purse is complete

Chain

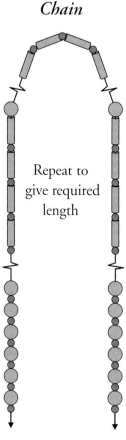

Repeat to
give required
length

Attach to purse

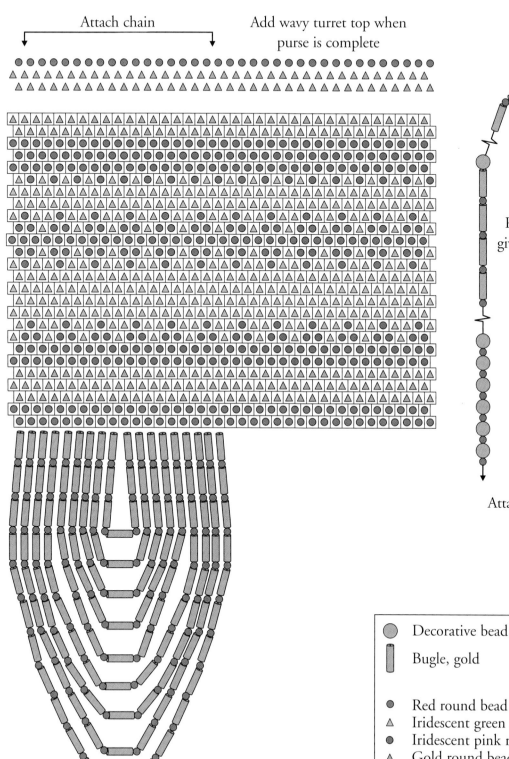

Decorative bead, gold

Bugle, gold

Red round bead
Iridescent green round bead
Iridescent pink round bead
Gold round bead

Antique diamond purse

MATERIALS AND EQUIPMENT

Weight of purse: 25 grams
Round beads, white (5 grams), iridescent pink
(5 grams), pale orange (5 grams), gold (5 grams),
dark brown (10 grams), antique gold (5 grams)

Bugle beads, bronze (10 grams)
18 large, decorative beads, gold
Reel of Nymo
Size 10 beading needle

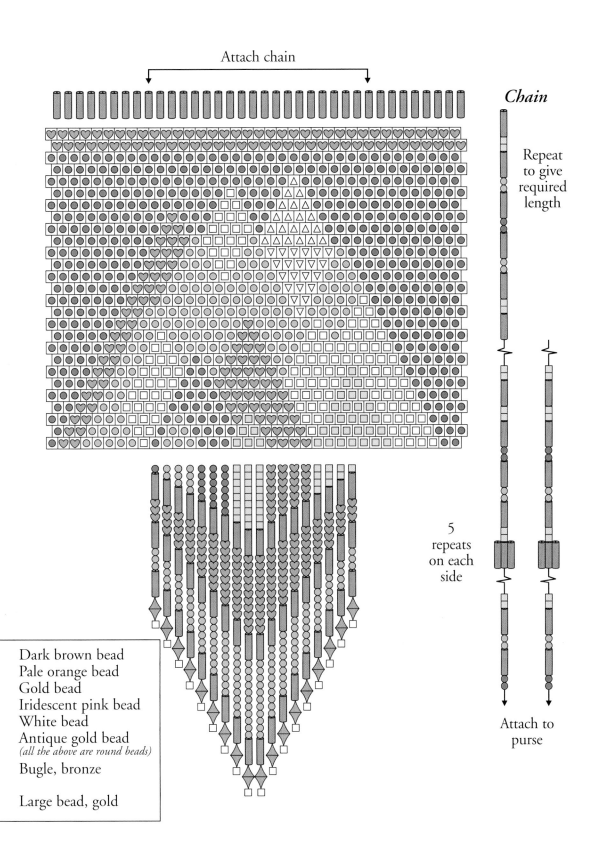

Attach chain

Chain

Repeat
to give
required
length

5
repeats
on each
side

Attach to
purse

- Dark brown bead
- Pale orange bead
- Gold bead
- Iridescent pink bead
- White bead
- Antique gold bead
  (all the above are round beads)
- Bugle, bronze
- Large bead, gold

Celtic black purse

MATERIALS AND EQUIPMENT

Weight of purse: 30 grams
Round beads, iridescent purple (5 grams),
black (15 grams), silver-lined (5 grams)
55 large, round silver beads, size 8

Bugles, black (5 grams)
19 decorative bells, silver
Reel of Nymo
Size 10 beading needle

Attach chain

Add looped top when
purse is complete

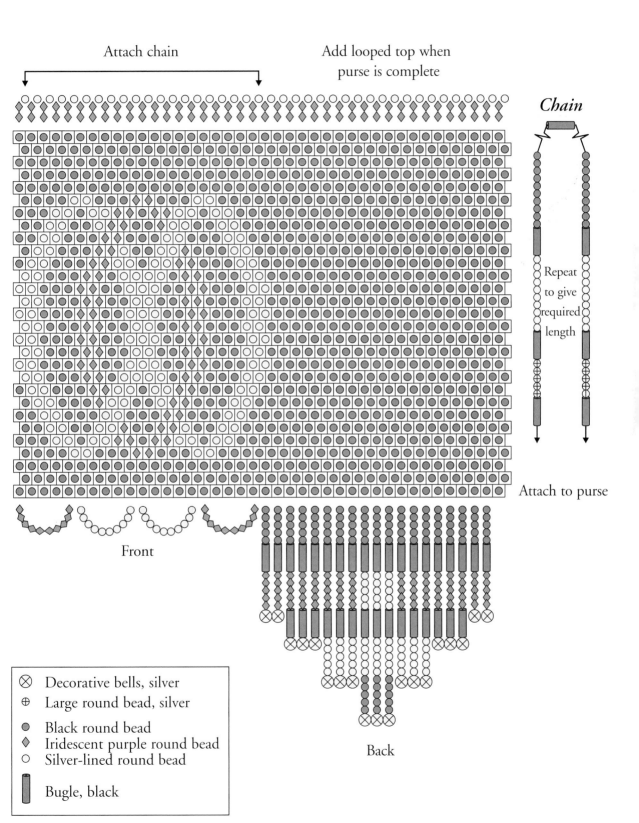

Chain

Repeat
to give
required
length

Attach to purse

Front

Back

⊗ Decorative bells, silver
⊕ Large round bead, silver
● Black round bead
◆ Iridescent purple round bead
○ Silver-lined round bead

▮ Bugle, black

Peacock tail purse

MATERIALS AND EQUIPMENT

Weight of purse: 30 grams
Round beads, metallic turquoise (5 grams),
iridescent turquoise (5 grams), bronze (5 grams),
iridescent pink (5 grams), gold (5 grams)

Bugles, metallic brown (10 grams)
Reel of Nymo
Size 10 beading needle

Attach chain

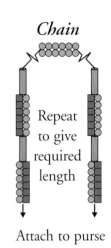

Chain

Repeat to give required length

Attach to purse

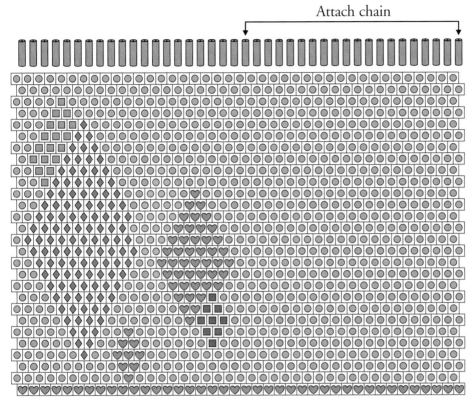

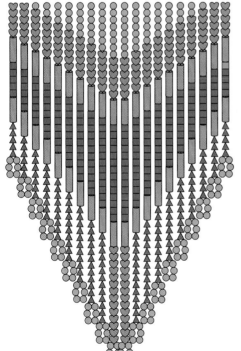

◆	Metallic dark turquoise round bead
■	Iridescent turquoise round bead
○	Iridescent pink round bead
♥	Brown round bead
●	Gold round bead
▲	Bronze round bead
▮	Bugle, metallic brown

CHAPTER 5

SQUARE STITCH PURSES

Square stitch enables you to produce straight lines horizontally and vertically, so I tend to work squares and rectangles into my patterns, leading to more abstract designs. A dramatic effect could be achieved by changing my subtle colour schemes to stronger, brighter shades, with immediate impact.

The square stitch grid is similar to that used in cross stitch and other needlework patterns – so can be used for the same kind of designs.

The following square stitch patterns should be worked vertically from the charts. Work the first row at the bottom left-hand corner, then work vertically upward to the top left-hand corner, then work the second vertical row. When the body of the purse is completed, the two ends are joined together, continuing to use the square stitch technique. The thread joining the rows of beads is along the top and bottom of the purse.

Blue and gold purse

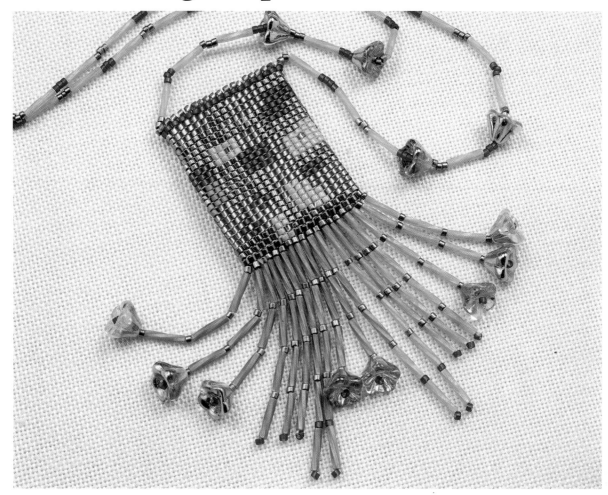

MATERIALS AND EQUIPMENT

Weight of purse: 15 grams
Delicas, purple (5 grams), metallic pink
(10 grams), matt beige (5 grams), ivory (5 grams),
copper (5 beads), gold (5 grams)

Bugle beads, twisted iridescent pink (5 grams)
12 decorative fluted beads, pink
Reel of Nymo
Size 10 beading needle

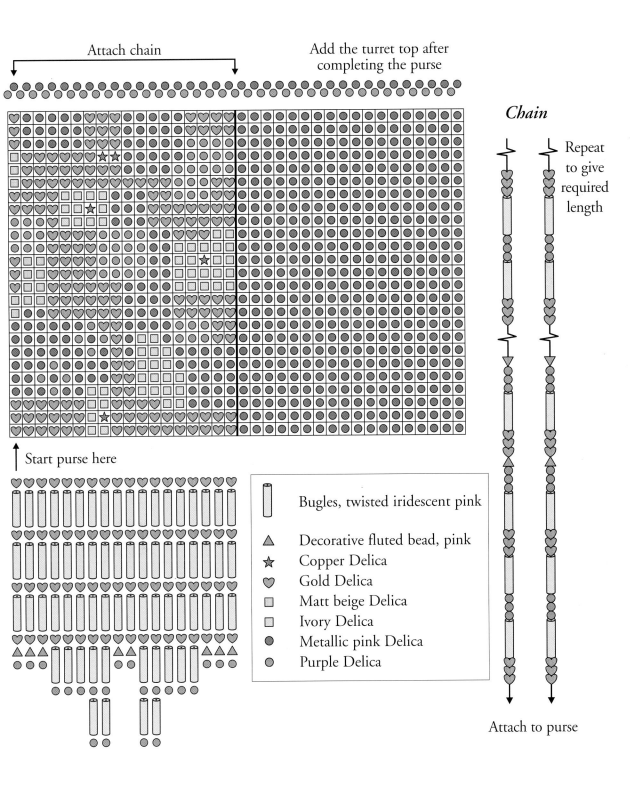

Attach chain

Add the turret top after
completing the purse

Chain

Repeat
to give
required
length

Start purse here

Bugles, twisted iridescent pink

△ Decorative fluted bead, pink
☆ Copper Delica
♡ Gold Delica
▢ Matt beige Delica
▢ Ivory Delica
● Metallic pink Delica
● Purple Delica

Attach to purse

STEP

1

Secure the first gold bead of the first row onto the thread and pick up the remaining 24 beads: 2 gold, 6 metallic pink, 2 matt beige, 3 gold, 3 purple, 2 gold, 3 matt beige, 3 gold.

STEP

2

Work back in square stitch, keeping the pattern correct. At the end of the row remember to thread the needle through the previous row and through the row you have just worked, see Steps 5 and 6 on page 19.

STEP

3

Complete the rows, following the chart. When you have completed the pattern, join the purse into a circle by putting the edges together and working in square stitch across the two edges.

Tip

If you find following the chart difficult the purse will still look attractive if worked in one multicoloured bead, or you could make up your own pattern.

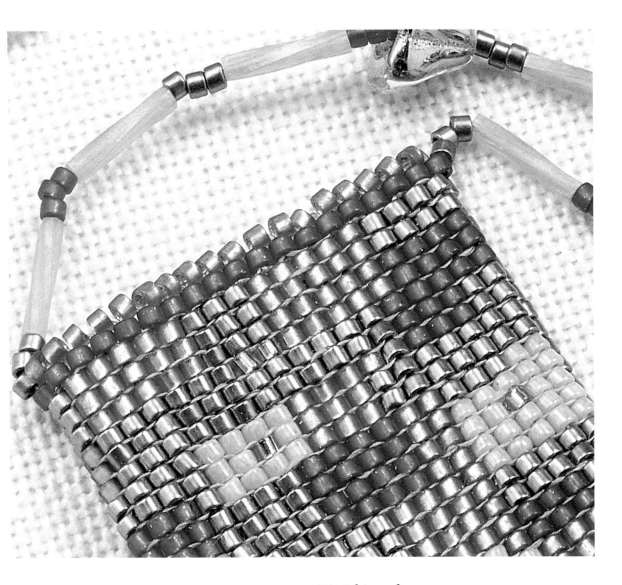

Decorative top

Complete the decorative top in turret stitch using a combination of the colours you have used in the purse. In my purse I used metallic pink and purple beads to complement the beads used in the body of the purse.

Finishing the purse

Stitch the bottom of the purse together. Select beads for the fringe and chain. Attach the fringe and work the chain. This is, perhaps, an opportunity to try out making your own beads for the chain, see page 43.

Iridescent green purse

MATERIALS AND EQUIPMENT

Weight of purse: 20 grams
Round beads, silver-lined (5 grams), iridescent
green (10 grams), iridescent clear (5 grams)
Bugles, twisted iridescent green (5 grams)

10 decorative iridescent green droplet beads
Reel of Nymo
Size 10 beading needle

Attach chain

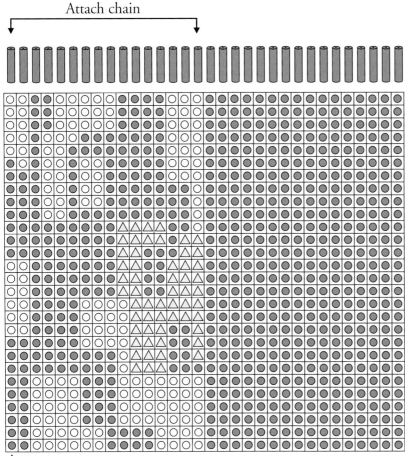

↑ Start here

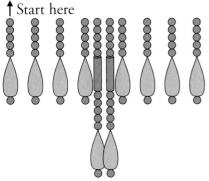

Chain

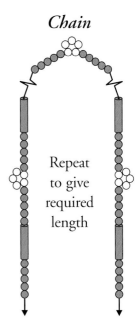

Repeat
to give
required
length

Attach to purse

○	Iridescent clear round bead
●	Iridescent green round bead
△	Silver-lined round bead
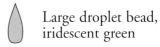	Large droplet bead, iridescent green
	Twisted bugle, iridescent green

Turquoise fantasy

MATERIALS AND EQUIPMENT

Weight of purse: 30 grams
Round beads, iridescent bronze (10 grams),
very pale turquoise (5 grams), matt turquoise
(5 grams), matt dark turquoise (5 grams),
light grey (5 grams), matt dark blue (5 grams),
metallic turquoise (5 grams)

Bugles, dark green (5 grams)
10 round decorative beads, gold
20 decorative gold beads
Reel of Nymo
Size 10 beading needle

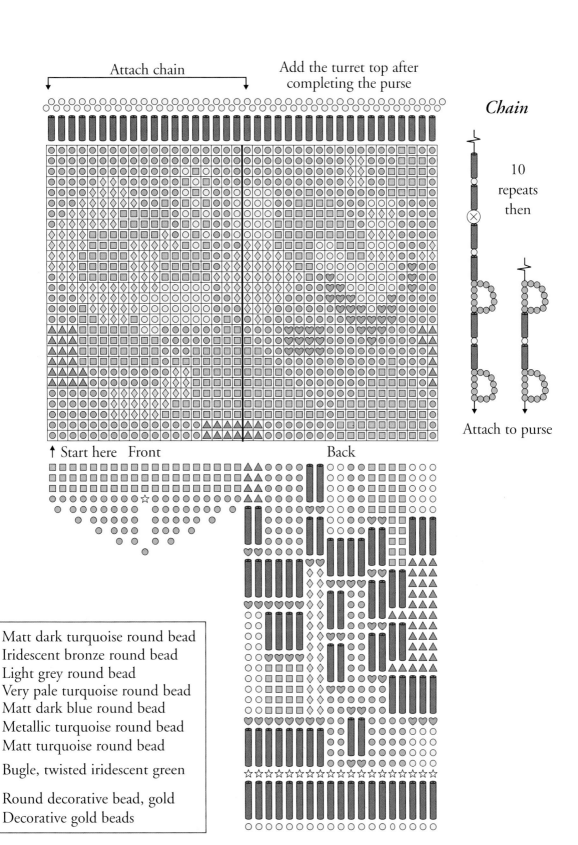

Attach chain

Add the turret top after completing the purse

Chain

10 repeats then

Attach to purse

↑ Start here   Front

Back

▲ Matt dark turquoise round bead
◉ Iridescent bronze round bead
◇ Light grey round bead
○ Very pale turquoise round bead
♥ Matt dark blue round bead
▣ Metallic turquoise round bead
▢ Matt turquoise round bead
█ Bugle, twisted iridescent green

⊗ Round decorative bead, gold
☆ Decorative gold beads

CHAPTER 6

PEYOTE STITCH PURSES

The peyote stitch purses I have included here range from the simple striped Amethyst glow purse to the intricate Peach glow purse.
My favourite is the Large soft mix purse. The large, soft-mix coloured beads give a multicoloured effect which goes well with a lot of colours I wear.

The Apricot diamond purse looks very effective with a dark, grey multicoloured background. Remember that you can change colours half way through working the purse, to create different designs for the back and front.

When working a peyote pattern, I find it easier to work the purse flat. Joining it together afterwards is easy.

Peyote charts can be worked in brick stitch provided you work across the pattern instead of up and down.

Amethyst glow purse

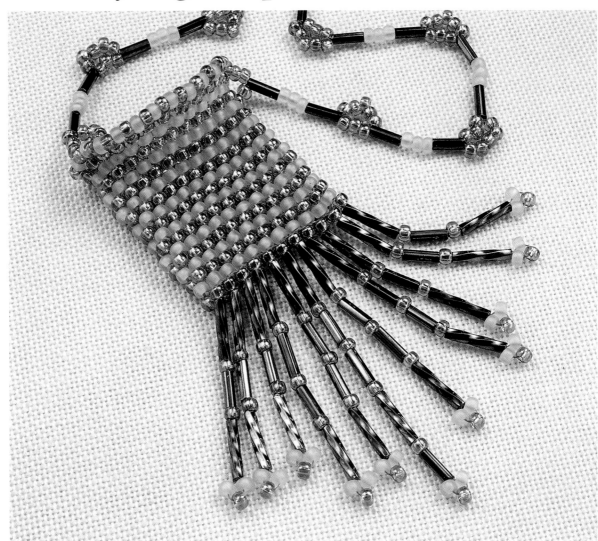

MATERIALS AND EQUIPMENT

Weight of purse: 20 grams
Round beads, light peach (10 grams) and
dark purple (10 grams)

Bugles, twisted iridescent purple (5 grams),
plain iridescent purple (5 grams)
Reel of Nymo
Size 10 beading needle

Begin
vertical
row 3
here

Attach chain

Add the turret top after
completing the purse

Chain

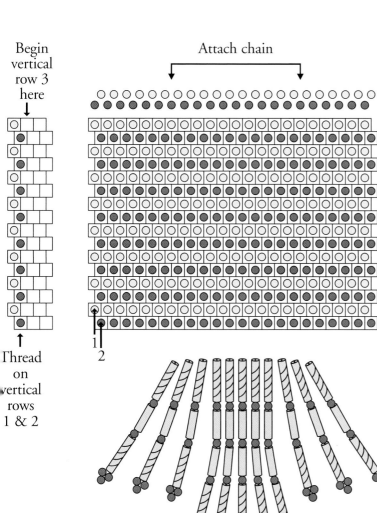

Thread
on
vertical
rows
1 & 2

1
2

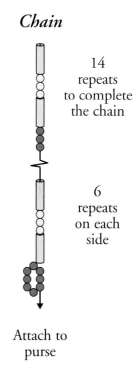

14
repeats
to complete
the chain

6
repeats
on each
side

Attach to
purse

	Twisted bugle, iridescent purple
	Bugle, iridescent purple
○	Light peach round bead
●	Dark purple round bead

To begin a peyote purse you need to pick up all the beads for the first two vertical rows in the correct order. The first two vertical rows of the chart for this purse are shown separately to illustrate the order in which the beads should be picked up onto the working thread.

Peyote with an even number of beads in each row is worked as demonstrated on page 21. At each end of the row, a bead is picked up that fits into place easily, see Step 2 on page 21. In odd-numbered peyote stitch, one end is worked as in Step 2 on page 21. The other end is worked as shown below.

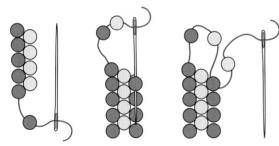

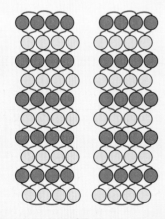

Tip
If you have worked the wrong number of rows the edges will not interlink, so you must either undo one row or work one more.

STEP

1

Pick up one dark bead and secure it with a double stitch through the bead. Pick up 15 beads, alternating the colours as indicated by the chart on page 77.

STEP

2

Pick up another bead the same colour as the last bead on your thread and work through the bead next to it, bead 15. Continue working using the technique described on page 21, picking up the same coloured bead all the way through the third vertical row.

STEP

3

Alternating the colours, complete the vertical rows. When you have worked all the flat peyote you will see that the right and left edges have alternating beads which will link together when the work is folded.

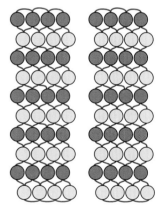

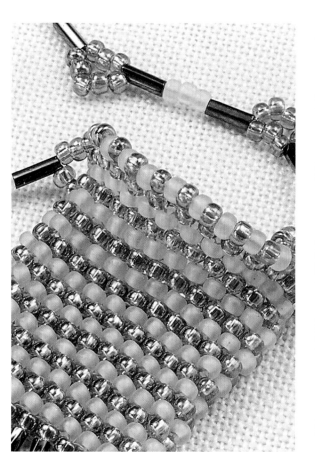

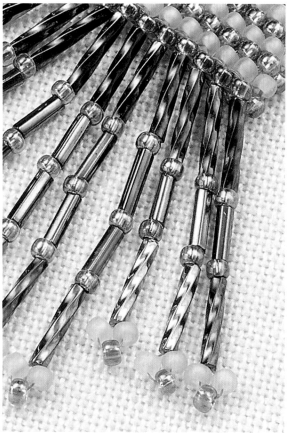

Finishing the purse

Join the edges by following the diagram (see right). The decorative top is a turret top with an extra bead to create a wavy effect, page 38. Join the bottom of the purse. Add the fringe and chain according to the pattern.

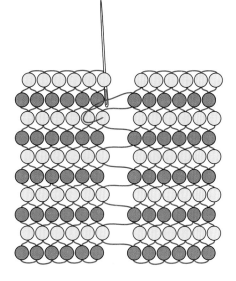

Green and gold purse

MATERIALS AND EQUIPMENT

Weight of purse: 25 grams
Round beads, size 8, gold (10 grams) and
dark green (10 grams)
Bugles, pink (5 grams)
27 gold decorative beads
Reel of Nymo
Size 10 beading needle

The pattern of this purse is the same as the basic purse. Treatment of the fringe is slightly more complicated. A short, looped fringe is added to the front with a longer, more ornate, fringe hanging from the back of the purse. The neck decoration is a turret.

Attach chain

Add the turret top after
completing the purse

Begin
vertical
row 3 here

Chain

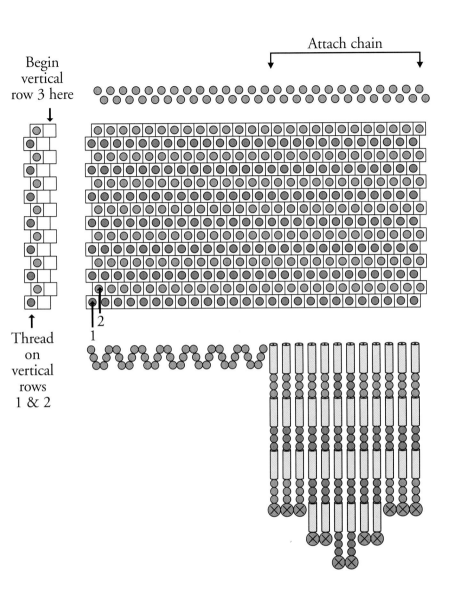

Thread
on
vertical
rows
1 & 2

1 2

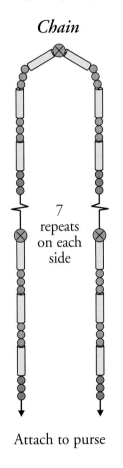

7
repeats
on each
side

Attach to purse

  Bugle, pink

○ Dark green round bead, size 8

● Gold round bead, size 8

⊗ Decorative bead, gold

Apricot diamond purse

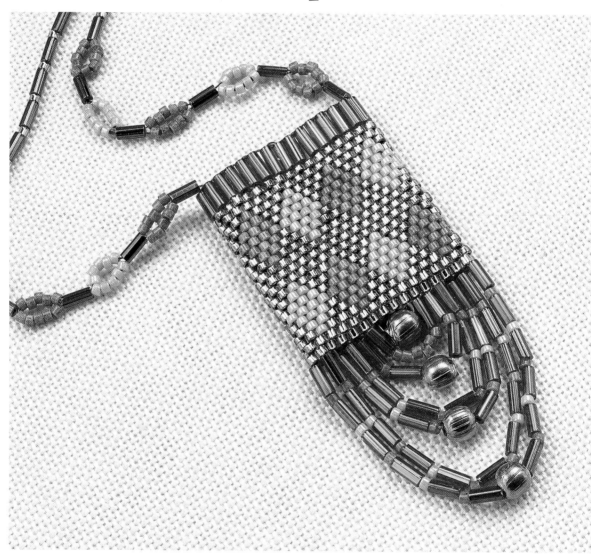

MATERIALS AND EQUIPMENT

Weight of purse: 10 grams
Delicas, gold (5 grams), dark orange (5 grams)
and light orange (5 grams)
Bugles, red (5 grams)

5 decorative beads, gold
Reel of Nymo
Size 10 beading needle

Begin
vertical
row 3
here

Attach chain

Chain

Repeat
to give
required
length

2
1

Thread
on
vertical
rows
1 & 2

Attach to purse

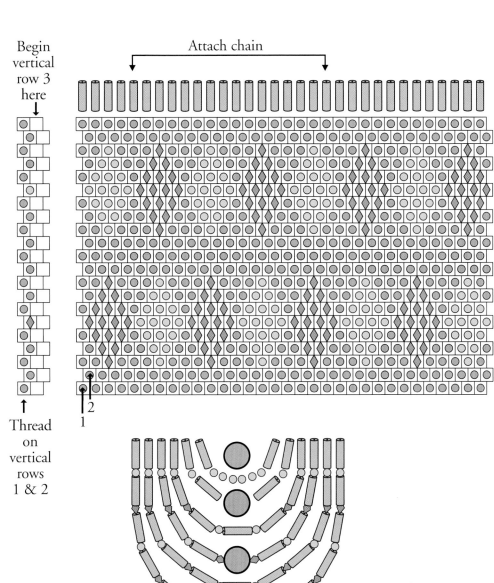

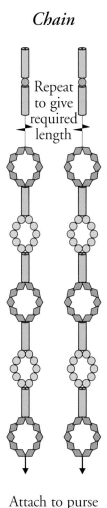

◆ Dark orange Delicas

○ Light orange Delicas

● Gold Delicas

⬤ Large decorative bead, gold

▯ Bugle, red

STEP

1

Pick up one gold bead and secure it with a double stitch through the bead. Pick up the rest of the beads for the first two vertical rows. The beads should be in the following order: 5G, 1D, 9G, 1L, 5G. There should be 21 beads in all.

STEP

2

Pick up two bugle beads and one G bead. Take the needle through the second gold bead on the thread before the bugle beads.

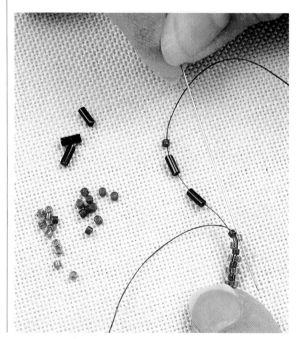

(Please note: this photograph illustrates adding bugle beads and does not follow the purse pattern.)

STEP

3

Pull up the work so that the bugle beads lie side by side and the two background beads at the base of the bugles are side by side. These bugles are at the top of the second and third vertical rows. One bugle is added at the top of each vertical row, after working through the previous bugle. The gold bead added in the diagram is the first bead of the third vertical row.

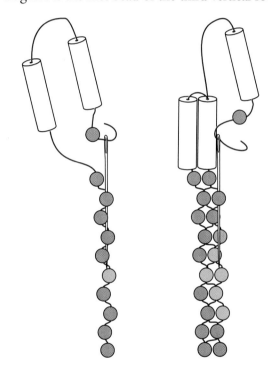

Bead Key
D = Dark orange Delica
L = Light orange Delica
G = Gold Delica

STEP
4

Continue working the vertical rows of the pattern across the chart. The table below shows the sequence of beads for each of the vertical rows that make up one section of the pattern.

Direction of work	Row	Bead colours	
Down	1	11G	These two vertical rows are worked together to begin the purse
Up	2	2G, 1L, 4G, 1D, 2G	Add 2 bugles
Down	3	2G, 2D, 3G, 2L, 2G	
Up	4	1G, 3L, 2G, 3D, 1G	Work through previous bugle then add 1 bugle
Down	5	1G, 4D, 1G, 4L, 1G	
Up	6	1G, 3L, 2 G 3D, 1G	Work through previous bugle then add 1 bugle
Down	7	2G, 1D, 4G, 1L, 2G	
Up	8	2G, 1L, 4G, 1D, 2G	Work through previous bugle then add 1 bugle

Finishing the purse

When complete, join the purse and the bugle beads into a circle. You will find that the two ends of the purse fit and you can join them together in the same way as for the basic purse. Add the fringe and the chain. The chain is worked with two needles to form decorative circles, see page 32.

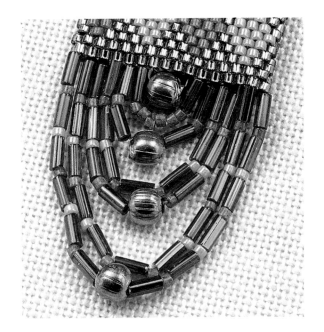

Soft mix purse

MATERIALS AND EQUIPMENT
Weight of purse: 10 grams
Delicas, gold (5 grams), dull gold (5 grams),
pink (5 grams) and dull brown (5 grams)
Bugles, twisted iridescent pink (5 grams)
Reel of Nymo
Size 10 beading needle

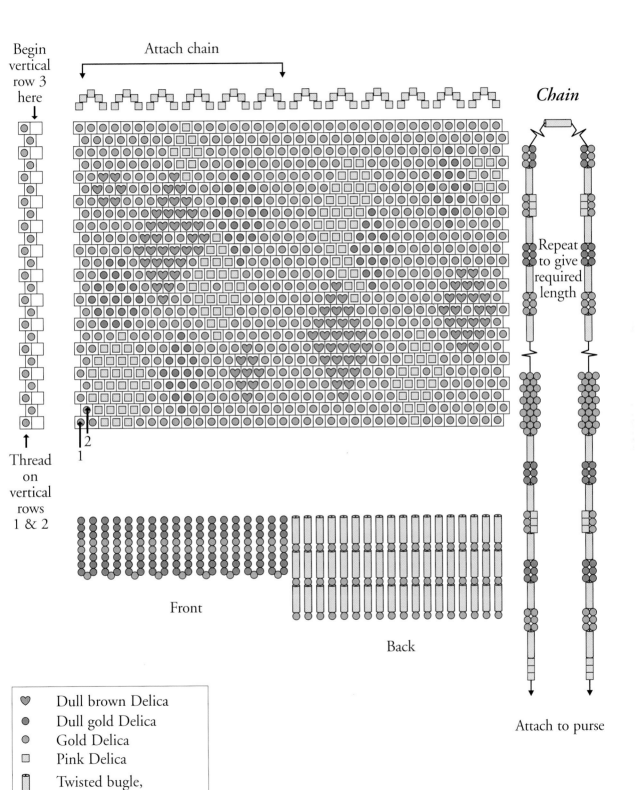

Begin vertical row 3 here

Attach chain

Chain

Repeat to give required length

Thread on vertical rows 1 & 2

1   2

Front

Back

Attach to purse

♥ Dull brown Delica
● Dull gold Delica
● Gold Delica
□ Pink Delica

Twisted bugle, iridescent pink

Large soft mix purse

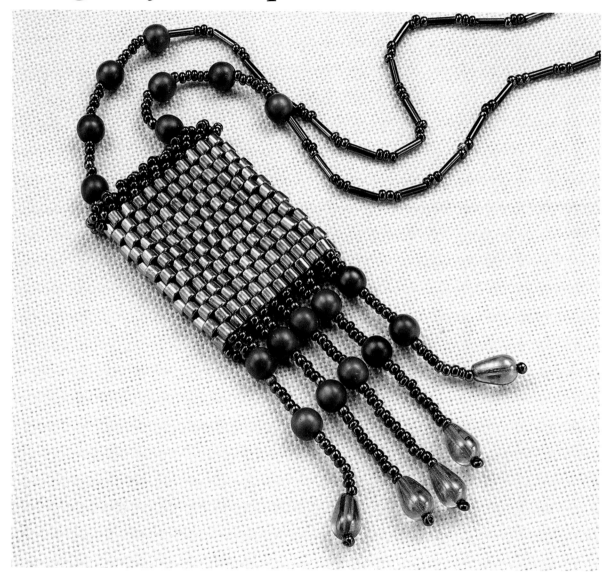

MATERIALS AND EQUIPMENT

Weight of purse: 20 grams
Delicas, iridescent purple (5 grams)
Bugles, iridescent purple (5 grams)
Delicas, soft mix, size 8 (2 tubes)

5 decorative drop beads, iridescent purple
18 large, round decorative beads, metallic green
Reel of Nymo
Size 10 beading needle

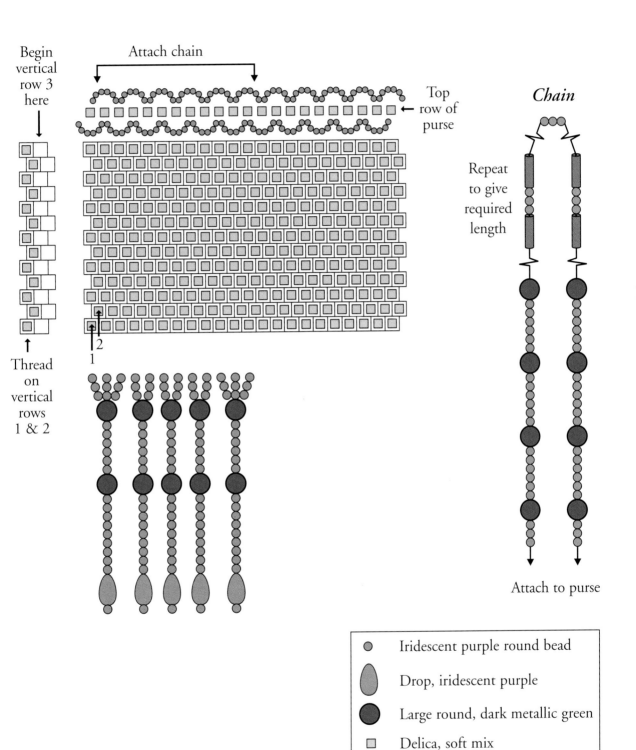

Begin
vertical
row 3
here

Thread
on
vertical
rows
1 & 2

Attach chain

Top
row of
purse

2
1

Chain

Repeat
to give
required
length

Attach to purse

○	Iridescent purple round bead
⬭	Drop, iridescent purple
⬤	Large round, dark metallic green
▫	Delica, soft mix
▮	Bugle, iridescent purple

Peach glow purse

MATERIALS AND EQUIPMENT

Weight of purse: 10 grams
Round beads, size 8, iridescent pale
mauve (5 grams)
Bugles, iridescent purple (5 grams)

Delicas, soft mix (5 grams), shell pink (5 grams)
Reel of Nymo
Size 10 beading needle

Add the turret top after
completing the purse

Attach chain

Chain

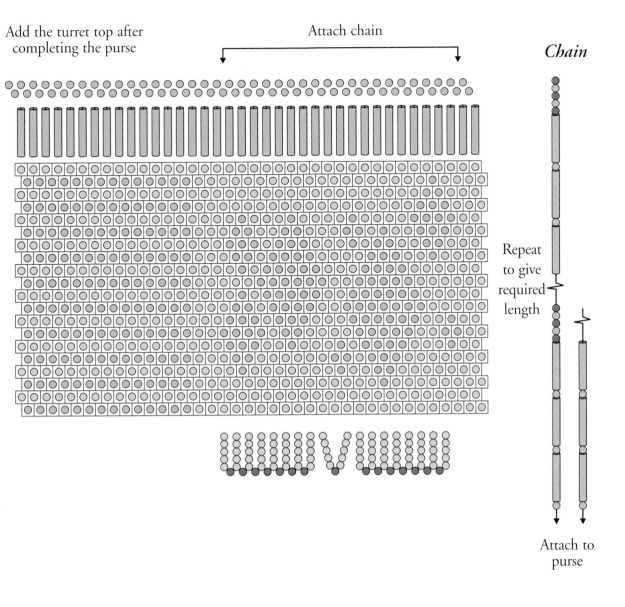

Repeat
to give
required
length

Attach to
purse

Bugle, iridescent purple

Iridescent pale mauve round beads

Delica, shell pink

Delica, soft mix

CHAPTER 7

NETTED PURSES

Netting purses are quicker to work than other types because part of the design is space. This method lends itself to extending the designs to make large purses, like evening bags, quickly. Add a colourful fabric lining to make the bag more attractive and useful.

These purses are worked in five-bead netting, as explained in Chapter Two (see page 22). For your first netted purse it is easier to work with three colours of beads. The netting shows up clearly and quickly as you work the purse. The different coloured beads help you to see where the needle goes next.

In all the designs shown you could change the colours half way through working the purse, to create a two-sided patttern. I also like the effect created by adding different sizes of beads, as in the Silver gem. The open structure of netting allows you to use bugle beads to replace the non-connecting beads in the net.

Three-tone purple purse

MATERIALS AND EQUIPMENT

Weight of purse: 15 grams
Round beads, iridescent purple (5 grams),
dull purple (10 grams) and silver-lined (5 grams)

Bugles, iridescent purple (5 grams)
Reel of Nymo
Size 10 beading needle

Attach chain

Chain

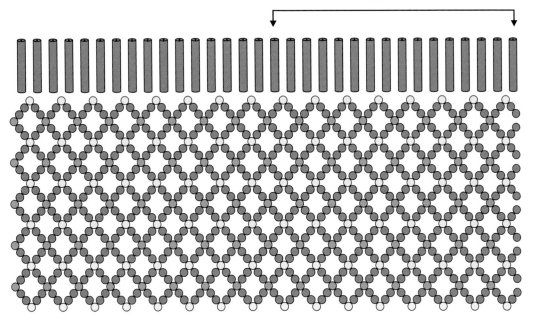

9 repeats,
miss off final
bugle so that
both sides
match

○ Iridescent purple round beads
● Dull purple round beads
○ Silver-lined round beads

▌ Bugle, iridescent purple

Attach to
purse

1

Work the neck with 36 bugle beads and 2m of Nymo thread. The instructions for making the neck are in Chapter 2, page 10. 36 beads make a good-sized netted purse.

Tip

A long thread will ensure that the thread will work all of the bugle beads, and some of the net, without a join. If threads have to be joined whilst working the neck, the holes in the beads will get full of thread. The holes need to be free to attach the net to the neck.

2

You can make the purse wider or narrower by using more or less bugle beads in the neck. If you decide to change the number of bugle beads in the neck, then keep to an even number of beads as you need two beads in the neck to complete the two rows that make up each net. Complete the neck but do not join it up into a circle at this stage. The purse is worked flat and joined into a circle when the netting is finished.

3

Using the thread left from working the neck, pick up six beads; starting with the clear silver-lined bead (A) pick up beads in the following order: A, B, B, C, B, B. Repeat this sequence until you have 36 beads on the thread. It is just coincidence that I used 36 bugle beads and 36 round beads.

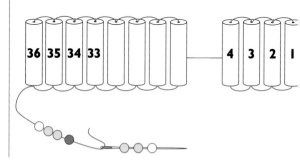

Tip

If you wish to make the purse longer you must add more round beads in multiples of six. This number of beads, six, applies to five-bead netting as explained in Chapter 2.

Bead Key
A = Silver-lined round bead
B = Dull purple round bead
C = Iridescent purple round bead

4

Once you have 36 beads on your thread, pull
them up close to the bugle bead. Count back
12 beads – the twenty-fifth bead from the top,
a silver-lined bead in this purse – and pass the
needle through it. Pull the thread gently so
that the beads form a loop.

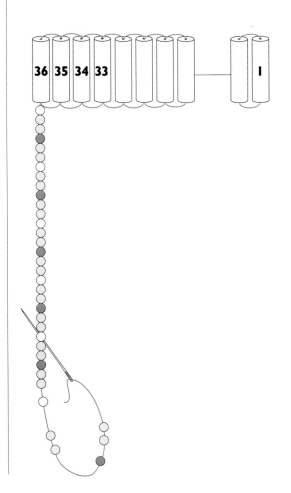

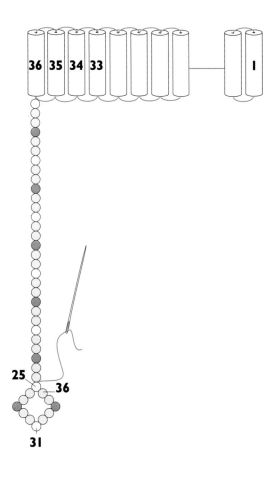

STEP
5

Keeping the colours correct, in this instance starting with a bead B, add five more beads (B, B, C, B, B). Take the needle through the nineteenth bead. The loop should always join through a silver-lined bead (A).

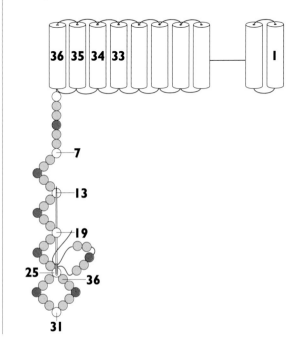

STEP
6

Continue adding five beads (B, B, C, B, B) and work the thread through the sixth bead back along the thread until you arrive at the first bead in the line.

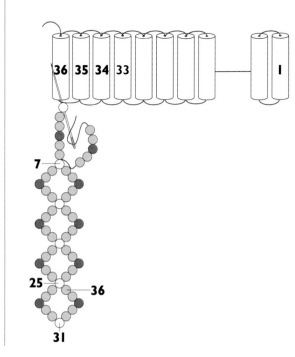

Bead Key

A = Silver-lined round bead
B = Dull purple round bead
C = Iridescent purple round bead

7

Take the needle up through the next bugle bead and down through the bugle bead next to it. This end of the net varies from the basic net stitch described in Chapter 2 because the netting has to be attached to the bugle beads which form the neck of the purse. With practice you will find that you can go through the round bead and the bugle bead in one action. You have now completed the two rows that make a net.

8

Bring the needle down through the bugle bead and add three round beads (A, B, B), Take the needle through the fourth bead (C) of the previous row of netting. This is the middle multicoloured bead of the previous five bead net. Add five beads in the following order (B, B, A, B, B) and work through the centre bead of the previous net. Repeat this process until you reach the last connecting bead.

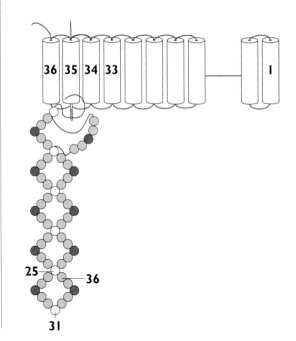

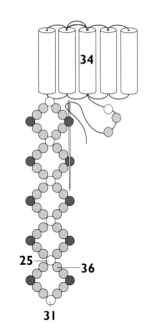

Tip
To keep the tension even, lay the work flat on the work surface, then pull up the thread through the first connecting bead.

STEP
9

Add eight beads (B, B, A, B, B, C, B, B), and work through the twelfth bead back. Continue adding five beads in the correct colours until you reach the bugle beads.

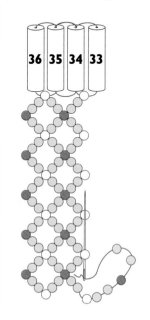

Bead Key

A = Silver-lined round bead

B = Dull purple round bead

C = Iridescent purple round bead

STEP
10

Go up through the next bugle bead, and down through one next to it. You are now ready to add three beads to start the next row of netting.

STEP
11

Continue the netting until you reach bugle bead one away from the edge of the neck. Work to the bottom of the purse as usual, but only add five beads instead of eight (B, B, A, B, B) at the end of the row. Fold the purse so that the two edges are close to one another, and work out which are the joining beads in the first and last rows. Take the needle through the joining bead (C bead) of the other edge of the purse.

STEP
12

Add two beads, (B, B), and pick up the joining bead (A) from the other edge following the dotted red line. Continue adding 2 beads and joining the edges all the way up the purse, following the dotted red line.

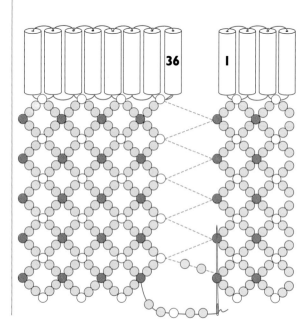

STEP
13

After working through the last round bead at the top, take the needle up through the last bugle bead on one edge of the purse and down through the first bugle bead of the other edge. Repeat this as many times as you can. When the holes become full, work through two or three other bugles to secure the thread. Thread the needle with the 13cm (½in) tail which you left at the beginning of the neck and work the thread into the netting to finish it off. You now have a circular net purse with a hole at the bottom which has to be joined.

EP

4

Fold the purse flat so that the points of the net at the bottom of the purse are on top of one another. Avoid placing the join in the bugle beads, which will be full of thread, at either side of the purse.

Joining a thread

Netting is open work, so any thread which crosses a space will show. The threads must follow the course of the netting. Thread into the purse, leaving a tail.

Take the needle round the netting twice, (see diagram). Do not thread through any of the common or connecting beads. The thread goes across the connecting bead and does not show.

Work through the beads in a diagonal line until the needle comes out where required.

Finish threads in the same way; work through the netting twice and go out through the netting diagonally, snip the end close to the beads.

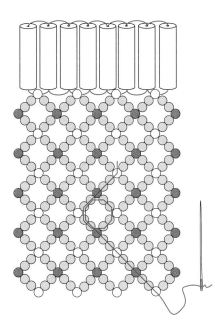

Joining the purse

Join a thread to the net (see left) bringing the thread out at the bottom of the purse on the righthand side, through the last joining bead (A bead) on the front of the purse. Go through the bead at the back of the purse, across again and through the bead at the front. Take the thread through the round beads to the next connecting point. Continue until the bottom of the purse is joined. When you have connected the last pair of common beads, secure the thread by working back into the netting.

The Chain

See the pattern for the sequence of beads needed for the chain. You can use your own design if you prefer. See page 31 for details about the best way to make up the chain and fix it to the body of the purse.

Two-tone purple purse

MATERIALS

Weight of purse: 20 grams
Bugles, twisted iridescent purple (10 grams)
Round beads, iridescent purple (10 grams)
and dull purple (10 grams)
Reel of Nymo
Size 10 beading needle

It is easy to change the colours worked on the front and back of these purses. The bugle beads could remain the same or change at the halfway (after 18 bugle beads). When working the net, change the colours of the net half way across the chart, making the back of the purse different from the front.

Attach chain

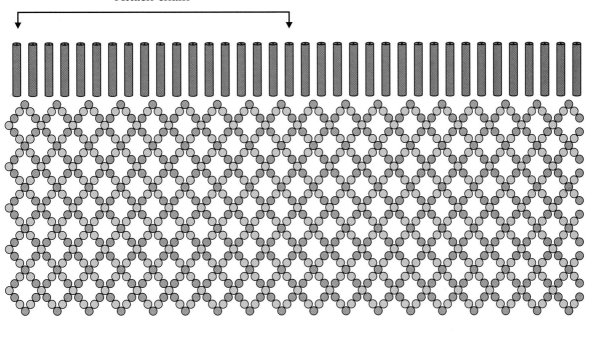

Chain

Repeat to give
required length.
Miss off final
bugle so that
both sides
match

Attach to purse

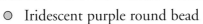

○ Iridescent purple round bead
● Dull purple round bead

Bugle, twisted iridescent purple

Black with a touch of red purse

MATERIALS AND EQUIPMENT
Weight of purse: 20 grams
Bugles, red (10 grams) and black (10 grams)
Round beads, red (10 grams) and
black (10 grams)
Reel of Nymo
Size 10 beading needle

Work this purse as shown in the chart. The extra net on one side of the purse acts as a decorative edge when the purse is joined up.

Attach chain

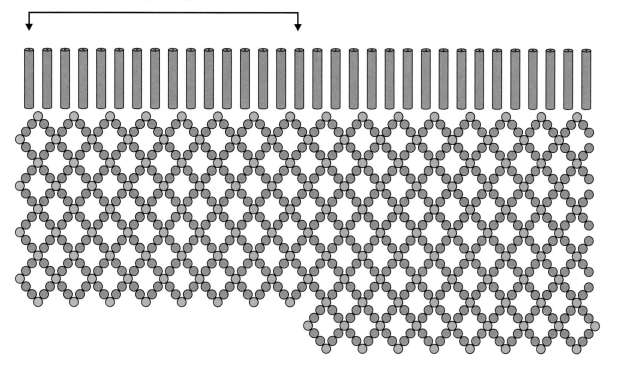

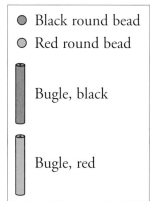

- ● Black round bead
- ● Red round bead

Bugle, black

Bugle, red

Chain

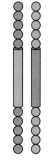

Secure two threads.
Repeat the patterns to
give required length.
Twist the two chains
together. secure the
ends without letting
go. (See Chapter 3,
page 32.)

Attach to
purse

The blues purse

MATERIALS AND EQUIPMENT
Weight of purse: 15 grams
Round beads, iridescent blue (10 grams) and dull blue (10 grams)

Bugles, twisted iridescent blue (10 grams)
Reel of Nymo
Size 10 beading needle

Attach chain

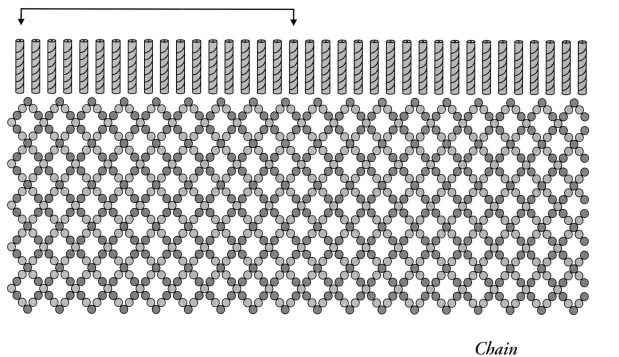

Chain

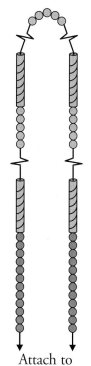

Repeat
to give
required
length

○ Iridescent blue round bead
● Dull blue round bead

Twisted bugle, iridescent blue

Attach to
purse

Silver gem purse

MATERIALS

Weight of purse: 15 grams
Round beads, silver-lined (5 grams)
56 large black decorative beads
(additional beads are needed for the chain)

Bugles, twisted silver (5 grams)
Reel of Nymo
Size 10 beading needle

Attach chain   Add turret top after completing purse

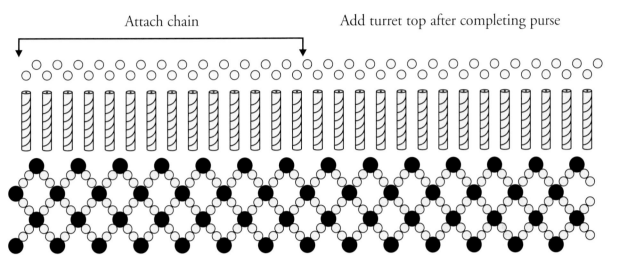

Chain

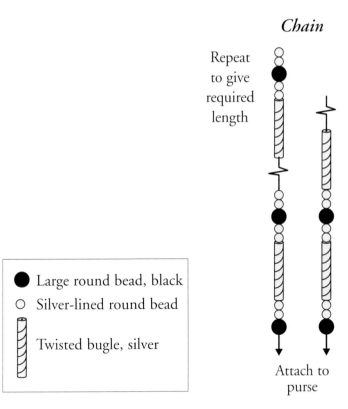

Repeat
to give
required
length

● Large round bead, black

○ Silver-lined round bead

▨ Twisted bugle, silver

Attach to
purse

CHAPTER 8

SQUARE NETTING PURSES

The technique used to make the sample of square netting in Chapter 2 is the basic foundation of any square netting purse. The size of one square depends on the number and size of beads used. Once you have decide how many squares are needed to make up the purse, you can easily calculate the number of large beads you need to fill all the squares. Remember that you will need additional beads for the chain and fringe.

When working your own designs, plan how the filling beads can be attached. Photocopy the plan then draw in, in pencil, how the threads can go so that you don't fill the pattern holes. There is a great deal of scope for planning a design within the mesh by using different shapes and colours of beads.

Once you have mastered the mesh it is quick and easy to produce a larger purse, which can be lined with fabric.

Gold mesh with black fill purse

MATERIALS AND EQUIPMENT

Weight of purse: 15 grams
Round beads, gold (10 grams)
90 large black round beads
(additional beads will be needed for the chain)

Bugles and decorative beads for chain
Reel of Nymo
Size 10 beading needle

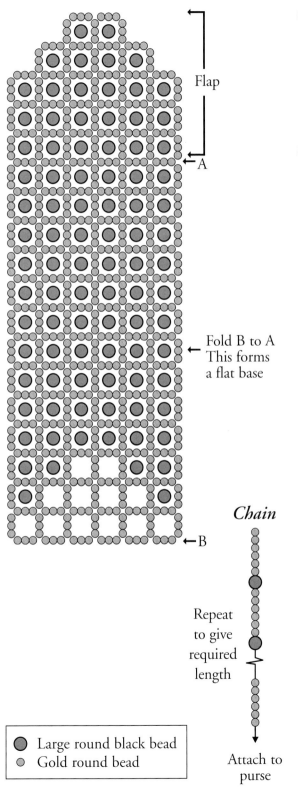

Flap

← A

Fold B to A
This forms
a flat base

← B

Chain

Repeat
to give
required
length

Attach to
purse

● Large round black bead
○ Gold round bead

1

Use small beads to work a piece of square netting, consisting of 16 x 6 squares (see page 26). Work two extra rows, one of four and one of two squares to form the flap of the purse.

STEP

2

Fill in the appropriate squares with the larger beads. The squares which will be underneath the flap do not need these decorative beads.

Finishing the purse

Fold the worked netting to form the purse. You will see that three beads, which form the sides of the back and front squares, lie alongside each other and can be stitched together. Take the thread through an inner bead, to avoid filling the hole, then stitch the next three pairs of beads together. Finish off securely. Attach the chain thread, add the chain beads. Secure the end firmly.

Golden eye purse

MATERIALS

Weight of purse: 15 grams
Round beads, gold (5 grams)
56 decorative beads, oval gold
(additional beads will be needed for the chain)
Reel of Nymo
Size 10 beading needle

In the all gold purse, oval beads have been used to fill the net. They look very attractive. Bugle beads could also be used or a mixture of round and tubular. Some holes have been left empty and this creates a pleasing pattern.

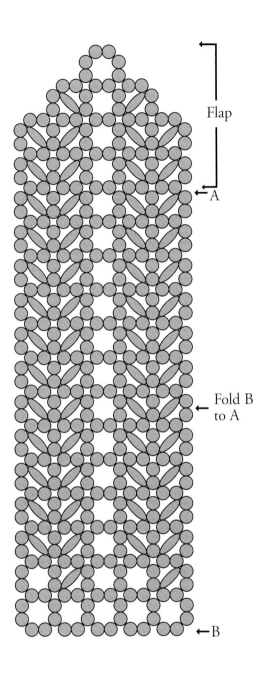

Flap

← A

Fold B
to A

← B

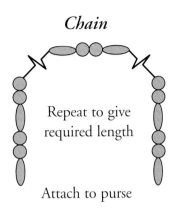

Chain

Repeat to give
required length

Attach to purse

○ Gold round beads
◗ Gold oval beads

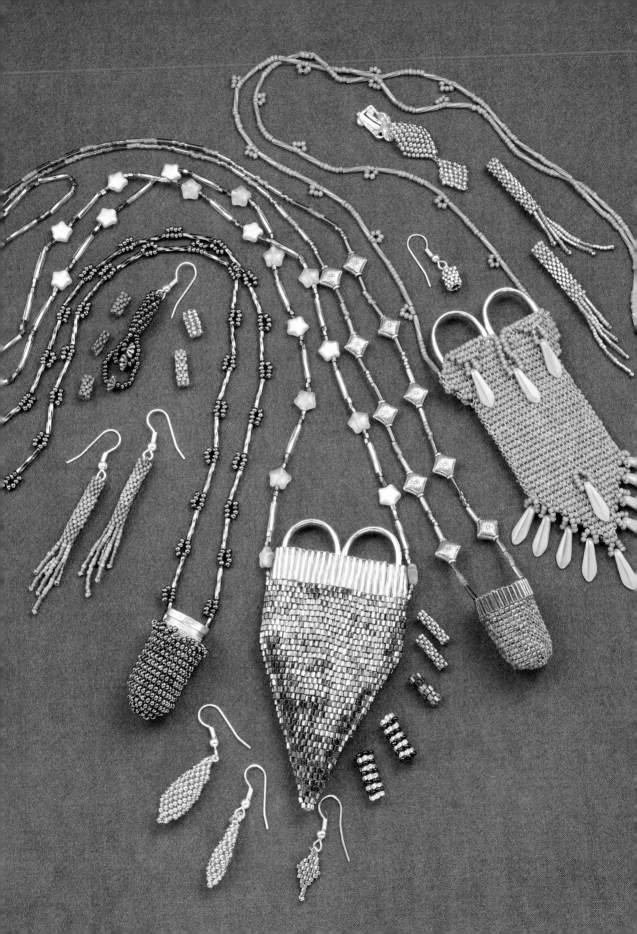

CHAPTER 9

VARIATIONS ON A THEME

In this chapter I have had fun working a few accessories. You can copy my designs or adapt them to your own needs.

Any of the purses in this book can be left open at the bottom and used as a scarf ring. The chain, which is essential to stop the ring from sliding down the scarf, needs to be the correct length to hold the scarf in position. Remember that the chain will need to be long enough to go over your head, unless you put a necklace fastener in it.

Earrings are very simple to make, in whatever stitch you choose. Most of the larger bead stockists sell earring findings.

Needlework accessories, like thimble and scissor cases, are practical and interesting to wear. At least you know where your thimble is if it isn't on your finger.

Tube earrings

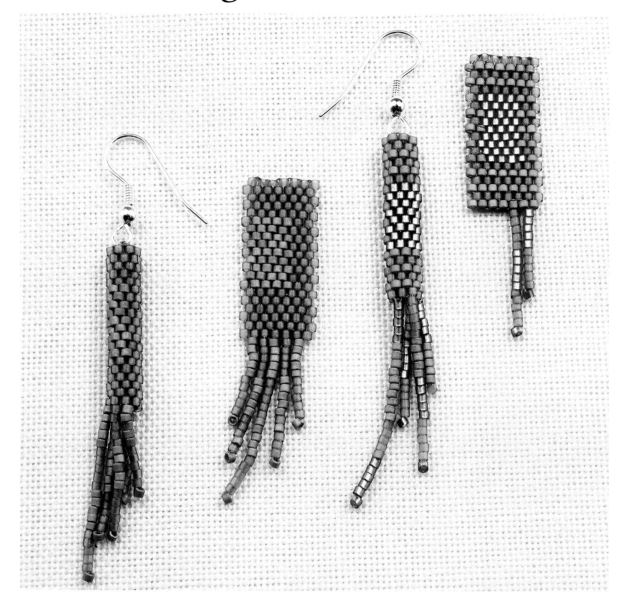

MATERIALS AND EQUIPMENT
Delicas, dull brown, dull green
(use up any leftover beads you have)
Reel of Nymo
Size 10 beading needle

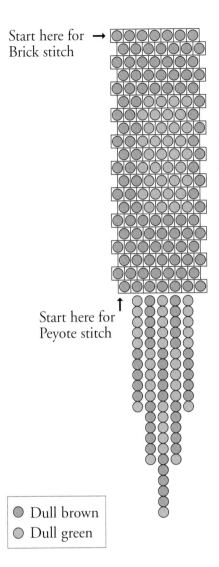

Start here for → Brick stitch

Start here for ↑ Peyote stitch

○ Dull brown
○ Dull green

For peyote stitch, begin with 20 beads on the thread. For brick stitch, attach seven beads together as you would to make a neck, see page 10.

For the second row add two beads with your first stitch, because you are working flat. Do this at the beginning of each row. Complete the flat work, following the chart. Add the fringe. Roll the flat piece into a circle and join up the earring as you would join a peyote or brick stitch purse.

Attaching the earrings to the findings

The method of attaching the earrings depends both on the finding and on the size of hole in the beads. The findings I use have a wire loop on which to hang the earring; this loop can be carefully opened and eased through a bead then closed again. If this is not possible, stitch the earring onto the finding loop with Nymo thread.

For these sample pairs I worked a stitch across the top of the earring. Look carefully at the finding and the pattern on the earring. You need to make sure that the pattern is hanging to the front and away from your face.

Attach a thread to one side of the earring and take it through the loop of the finding. Attach it to the other side of the circle. Repeat this several times. Buttonhole over the threads to make them look neat. Finish off the thread in the beads.

This pattern can be worked in either brick stitch or peyote stitch. The pattern has arrows indicating where you should begin, depending on which stitch you decide to use. If you decide to use peyote stitch remember to pick up the first two vertical rows of beads together. The earrings are worked flat and then joined after working. For each pair I have worked one earring in peyote and one in brick stitch. Can you tell the difference?

Diamond earrings

MATERIALS AND EQUIPMENT

Round beads, iridescent pink
(use up any leftover beads you have)
Reel of Nymo
Size 10 beading needle

Start here →

Start here →

Start here →

Start here →

○ Iridescent pink
  round beads

STEP 1

Attach 10 beads together using brick stitch. Work back across the row, adding nine beads. Add eight beads for the third row. Reduce each row by one bead.

STEP 2

Continue working the rows, reducing the number of beads by one each row until you have reached the last possible row when you can add only one bead. You should have a flat triangular shape. Take the thread through the beads to the point where you began. If you haven't enough thread secure a new thread at this point.

STEP 3

Turn the work round and add nine beads to this side. Work rows of brick stitch as above, reducing the number of beads by one for each row. Continue until you reach the point where you have secured the last bead. You should now have a diamond shape.

Attaching the earrings to the findings

Attach the last bead to the finding. The work can be left as a flat diamond shaped earring, or join the two sides at the back by stitching the beads at the tip of the diamond points together. Work the thread through the beads three times, joining them together securely.

A further alternative is to add spacing beads between the tips of the diamond before they are stitched together. Finish the thread off.

Variations

There are other variations using this basic pattern. Make a series of diamond shapes starting the first with 10 beads, the second with eight beads and the third with six beads. Join the three diamonds together, one below the other to make the earring.

Strawberry scissor case

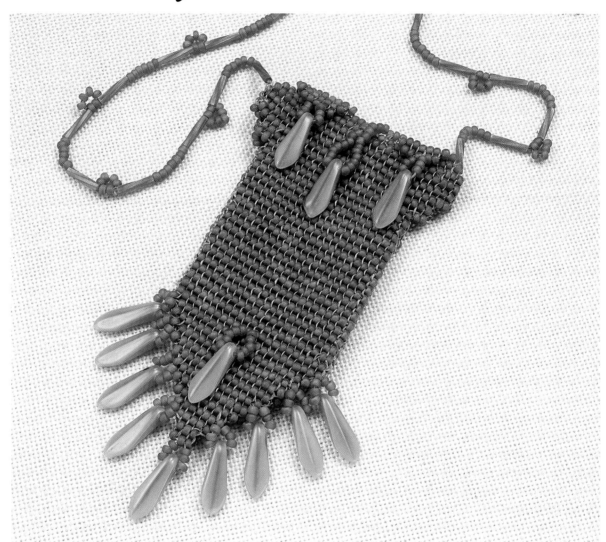

MATERIALS
Weight of case: 25 grams
Bugles, pink (5 grams)
Round beads, multicoloured pink (20 grams)
12 decorative droplet beads, pink
Reel of Nymo
Size 10 beading needle

Finishing the purse
Place the two halves of the purse together and stitch them together using square stitch through the beads which lie on top of one another down the edges. Attach the decorative beads. Fold over the flaps and secure them to the top piece of the case with a stitch through the beads. Attach the chain.

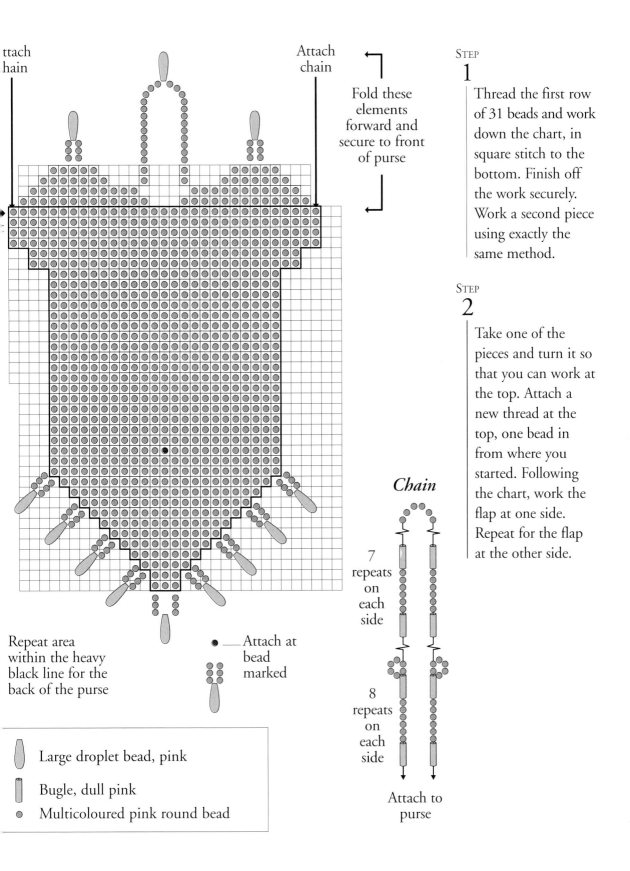

ttach
hain

Attach
chain

Fold these
elements
forward and
secure to front
of purse

1

Thread the first row
of 31 beads and work
down the chart, in
square stitch to the
bottom. Finish off
the work securely.
Work a second piece
using exactly the
same method.

STEP
2

Take one of the
pieces and turn it so
that you can work at
the top. Attach a
new thread at the
top, one bead in
from where you
started. Following
the chart, work the
flap at one side.
Repeat for the flap
at the other side.

Chain

7
repeats
on
each
side

8
repeats
on
each
side

Attach to
purse

Repeat area
within the heavy
black line for the
back of the purse

Attach at
bead
marked

Large droplet bead, pink

Bugle, dull pink

Multicoloured pink round bead

Shimmering gold scissors case

MATERIALS AND EQUIPMENT

Weight of case: 25 grams
Bugle, twisted gold (5 grams)
Square-cut iridescent gold beads (20 grams)

18 decorative pearl star beads
Reel of Nymo
Size 10 beading needle

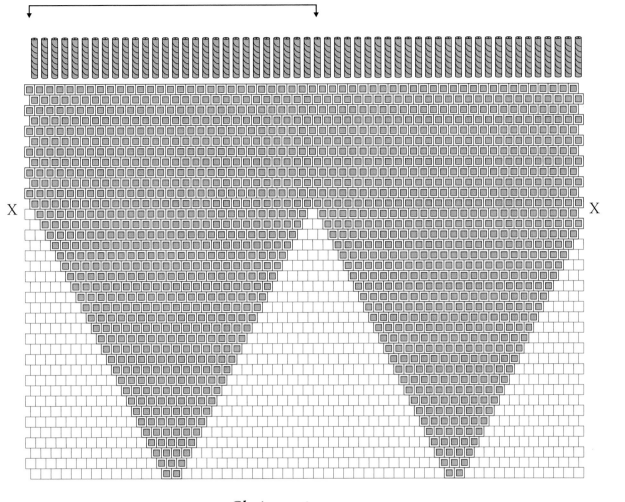

Attach chain

X   X

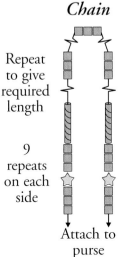

Chain

Repeat
to give
required
length

9
repeats
on each
side

Attach to
purse

Square-cut
iridescent
gold bead

Twisted
bugle, gold

Decorative
pearl star bead

STEP
1

Use the bugle beads to make a neck for the
case, see page 10. Join up the neck.

STEP
2

Work the case in brick stitch in the round to
point X. Then, complete the two sides
separately. Decrease the number of beads in a
row, by leaving off one bead at the beginning
and end of each row. Join the two halves
together. Attach the chain.

Metallic green thimble holder

MATERIALS AND EQUIPMENT
Weight of case: 5–10 grams
Bugles, twisted iridescent green (5 grams)
Round beads, iridescent green (10 grams)
Reel of Nymo
Size 10 beading needle

My thimble is an essential item of my needlework equipment. I am lost without it, but I have frequently been known to misplace it. A thimble holder is not only pretty but it serves the useful purpose of keeping my thimble readily to hand.

Don't make the thimble holder too tight. The thimble needs to be able to drop easily into the holder. If it is too tight the thimble could pop out and get lost.

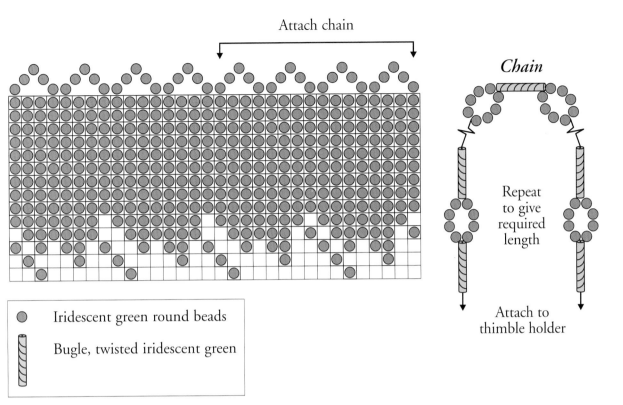

Iridescent green round beads

Bugle, twisted iridescent green

1

Thread 32 beads onto the thread. Place this row round the top of your thimble to see if it joins comfortably. Adjust the number of beads to give the right fit.

STEP
2

Join the beginning to the end of the row. Work a total of nine rows in the round. In the tenth row, begin decreasing to shape the bottom. Do this by adding seven beads then miss stitching into the next bead in the row above, add another seven beads and miss one. Repeat this twice more. You will have missed out every eighth bead, so have reduced the row evenly from 32 to 28. Where you miss a bead, pull the work up firmly to close any gaps.

STEP
3

In row 11, decrease by four again. Add six, miss one; do this four times in all leaving you with 24 beads in the row. In the twelfth row decrease by eight. Add two, miss one; do this eight times in all leaving 16 beads in the row. In the thirteenth row, decrease by eight. Add one, miss one; do this eight times leaving eight beads in the row. In the fourteenth row, decrease by four. Add one, miss one; repeat this four times.

STEP
4

Take the needle through the last four beads and pull the thread up tight. Finish off the thread securely in the beads. Decorate the top. Add the chain.

Orange glow thimble holder

MATERIALS AND EQUIPMENT

Weight of case: 10 grams
Bugles, bronze (5 grams)
Delicas, gold (5 grams) and orange (5 grams)

100 decorative beads, gold
Reel of Nymo
Size 10 beading needle

Attach chain

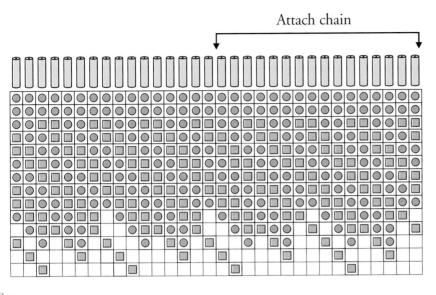

Chain

Repeat
to give
required
length

5
repeats
on each
side

Attach to
thimble
holder

STEP
1

Work 32 bugle beads as a neck, see page 10.
Before joining up, check that they will fit
round your thimble. If it is necessary to add
beads then they must be added in multiples of
four in order to maintain the pattern. Join up
the neck into a circle.

STEP
2

Attach the first row in square stitch using the
joining thread of the bugles to stitch into.
Work a total of nine rows. The first two rows
are plain, gold in the sample. The next seven
rows are patterned, two gold beads alternating
with two orange beads, each row being offset
by one bead. This gives the spiral effect.

STEP
3

Shape the bottom by decreasing from tenth
row as in the previous pattern. There may be
some slight distortion of the pattern as you
reduce the numbers of beads. Add the chain.

◆ Gold decorative bead

▯ Bronze bugle

◉ Gold Delica

▫ Orange Delica

Scarf holder

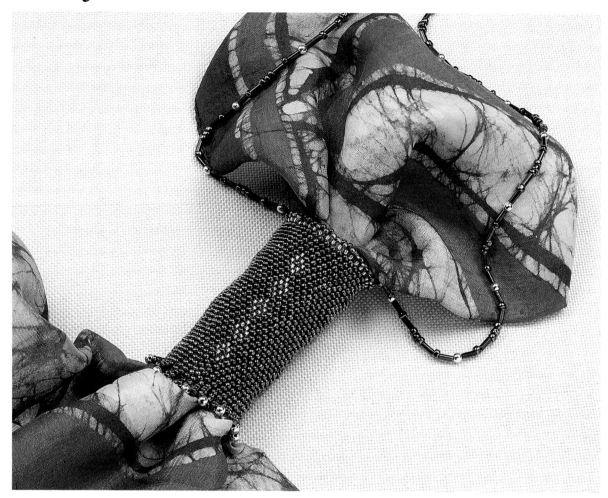

MATERIALS AND EQUIPMENT

Weight of holder: 20 grams
Bugles, iridescent purple (5 grams)
Round beads, iridescent purple (5 grams),
metallic blue (15 grams), silver (5 grams)

39 size 8 round beads
Reel of Nymo
Size 10 beading needle

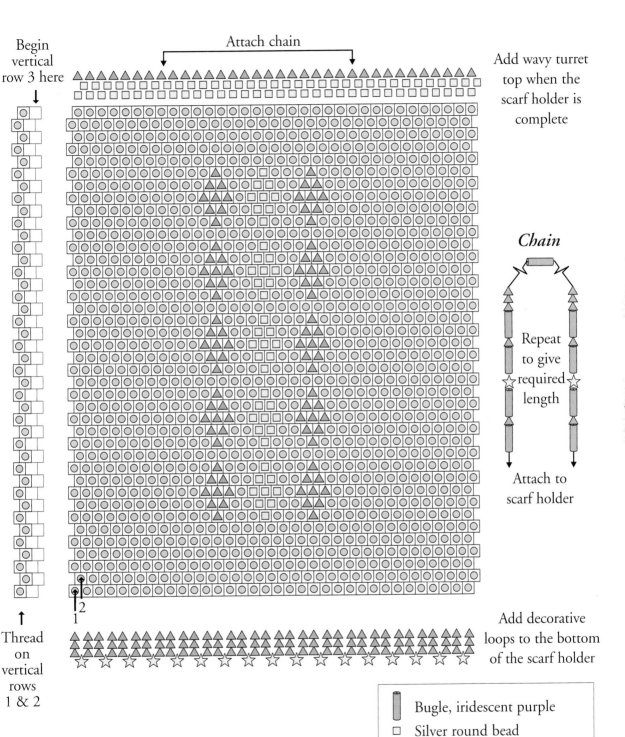

Begin
vertical
row 3 here
↓

Attach chain

Add wavy turret
top when the
scarf holder is
complete

Chain

Repeat
to give
required
length

Attach to
scarf holder

Thread
on
vertical
rows
1 & 2

1 2

Add decorative
loops to the bottom
of the scarf holder

Bugle, iridescent purple
□ Silver round bead
△ Iridescent purple round bead
○ Metallic blue round bead
☆ Size 8 silver bead

My scarf holder started as my first flat peyote sampler. Because I had no idea how many beads to start with or how long it would be, I started with 40 beads making the first two rows. I worked the set of iridescent diamonds, which hardly show, a set of silver diamonds down the centre and another set of iridescent diamonds. When I felt that I had worked enough to know the stitch, I joined it up into a circle. It seemed too long for a purse so I left the bottom open to take a scarf.

Decorative top

The top is finished with a wavy turret, see page 38. The bottom has loops of six small beads with one larger, size 8 silver bead in the centre of the loop.

Adding the chain

A chain is added to keep the scarf holder in position. Without the chain the beads would slide down the scarf. Any purse can be used as a scarf holder as long as the bottom is left open.

GALLERY

Photograph overleaf on the left.

Starting with the black purse top left and
working round in a clockwise direction:
Marisa Merritt, Clare Walsh, Sara MacPherson,
Clare Walsh, Zoë Donaldson, Linda Settle.

Photograph overleaf on the right.

Starting with the top red and black purse,
working in a clockwise direction: Grace Waller,
Grace Waller, Elizabeth Temple, Grace Waller.

ABOUT THE AUTHOR

Enid Taylor was born and educated in Skipton, Yorkshire. After training as a Home Economics teacher in London, she taught in schools, college and teacher training college for 24 years.

In 1982, she left the teaching profession to start her own business. Her first venture was a Craft Studio where she taught lacemaking, spinning and needlework, and visiting teachers gave weekend courses. The Studio also provided an outlet for a wide range of British handicrafts as well as being a popular tea-room. As a second venture she set up a sucessful embroidery and craft shop in Scarborough.

Enid has arranged several lace and embroidery exhibitions at Scarborough Art Gallery. She is also involved in the organization of the annual Fashion and Embroidery Exhibition run by Madeira Threads (UK) in Harrogate.

Enid and her husband Terry now live in the countryside near Scarborough. She does some teaching and consultancy work, and finds time for needlework in between gardening and helping her son who runs a local business.

GMC PUBLICATIONS

BOOKS

Crafts

Bargello: A Fresh Approach to Florentine Embroidery *Brenda Day*
Beginning Picture Marquetry *Lawrence Threadgold*
Blackwork: A New Approach *Brenda Day*
Celtic Cross Stitch Designs *Carol Phillipson*
Celtic Knotwork Designs *Sheila Sturrock*
Celtic Knotwork Handbook *Sheila Sturrock*
Celtic Spirals and Other Designs *Sheila Sturrock*
Celtic Spirals Handbook *Sheila Sturrock*
Complete Pyrography *Stephen Poole*
Creating Made-to-Measure Knitwear: A Revolutionary Approach to
  Knitwear Design *Sylvia Wynn*
Creative Backstitch *Helen Hall*
Creative Log-Cabin Patchwork *Pauline Brown*
Creative Machine Knitting *GMC Publications*
The Creative Quilter: Techniques and Projects *Pauline Brown*
Cross-Stitch Designs from China *Carol Phillipson*
Cross-Stitch Floral Designs *Joanne Sanderson*
Decoration on Fabric: A Sourcebook of Ideas *Pauline Brown*
Decorative Beaded Purses *Enid Taylor*
Designing and Making Cards *Glennis Gilruth*
Designs for Pyrography and Other Crafts *Norma Gregory*
Dried Flowers: A Complete Guide *Lindy Bird*
Exotic Textiles in Needlepoint *Stella Knight*
Glass Engraving Pattern Book *John Everett*
Glass Painting *Emma Sedman*
Handcrafted Rugs *Sandra Hardy*
Hobby Ceramics: Techniques and Projects for Beginners
  Patricia A. Waller
How to Arrange Flowers: A Japanese Approach to English Design
  Taeko Marvelly
How to Make First-Class Cards *Debbie Brown*
An Introduction to Crewel Embroidery *Mave Glenny*
Machine-Knitted Babywear *Christine Eames*
Making Decorative Screens *Amanda Howes*
Making Fabergé-Style Eggs *Denise Hopper*
Making Fairies and Fantastical Creatures *Julie Sharp*
Making Hand-Sewn Boxes: Techniques and Projects *Jackie Woolsey*
Making Mini Cards, Gift Tags & Invitations *Glennis Gilruth*
Native American Bead Weaving *Lynne Garner*
New Ideas for Crochet: Stylish Projects for the Home *Darsha Capaldi*

Papercraft Projects for Special Occasions *Sine Chesterman*
Papermaking and Bookbinding: Coastal Inspirations *Joanne Kaar*
Patchwork for Beginners *Pauline Brown*
Pyrography Designs *Norma Gregory*
Rose Windows for Quilters *Angela Besley*
Silk Painting for Beginners *Jill Clay*
Sponge Painting *Ann Rooney*
Stained Glass: Techniques and Projects *Mary Shanahan*
Step-by-Step Pyrography Projects for the Solid Point Machine
  Norma Gregory
Stitched Cards and Gift Tags for Special Occasions *Carol Phillipson*
Tassel Making for Beginners *Enid Taylor*
Tatting Collage *Lindsay Rogers*
Tatting Patterns *Lyn Morton*
Temari: A Traditional Japanese Embroidery Technique *Margaret Ludlow*
Three-Dimensional Découpage: Innovative Projects for Beginners
  Hilda Stokes
Trompe l'Oeil: Techniques and Projects *Jan Lee Johnson*
Tudor Treasures to Embroider *Pamela Warner*
Wax Art *Hazel Marsh*

Dolls' Houses and Miniatures

1/12 Scale Character Figures for the Dolls' House
  James Carrington
Americana in 1/12 Scale: 50 Authentic Projects
  Joanne Ogreenc & Mary Lou Santovec
The Authentic Georgian Dolls' House *Brian Long*
A Beginners' Guide to the Dolls' House Hobby *Jean Nisbett*
Celtic, Medieval and Tudor Wall Hangings
  in 1/12 Scale Needlepoint *Sandra Whitehead*
Creating Decorative Fabrics: Projects in 1/12 Scale *Janet Storey*
Dolls' House Accessories, Fixtures and Fittings *Andrea Barham*
Dolls' House Furniture: Easy-to-Make Projects in 1/12 Scale
  Freida Gray
Dolls' House Makeovers *Jean Nisbett*
Dolls' House Window Treatments *Eve Harwood*
Edwardian-Style Hand-Knitted Fashion for 1/12 Scale Dolls
  Yvonne Wakefield

BOOKS (CONT.)

Dolls' Houses and Miniatures

Making 1/12 Scale Wicker Furniture for the Dolls' House
Sheila Smith
Making Miniature Chinese Rugs and Carpets *Carol Phillipson*
Making Miniature Food and Market Stalls *Angie Scarr*
Making Miniature Gardens *Freida Gray*
Making Miniature Oriental Rugs & Carpets *Meik & Ian McNaughton*
Making Miniatures: Projects for the 1/12 Scale Dolls' House
Christiane Berridge
Making Period Dolls' House Accessories *Andrea Barham*
Making Tudor Dolls' Houses *Derek Rowbottom*
Making Upholstered Furniture in 1/12 Scale *Janet Storey*
Making Victorian Dolls' House Furniture *Patricia King*
Medieval and Tudor Needlecraft: Knights and Ladies
in 1/12 Scale *Sandra Whitehead*
Miniature Bobbin Lace *Roz Snowden*
Miniature Crochet: Projects in 1/12 Scale *Roz Walters*
Miniature Embroidery for the Georgian Dolls' House *Pamela Warner*
Miniature Embroidery for the Tudor and Stuart Dolls' House
Pamela Warner
Miniature Embroidery for the 20th-Century Dolls' House
Pamela Warner
Miniature Embroidery for the Victorian Dolls' House *Pamela Warner*
Miniature Needlepoint Carpets *Janet Granger*
More Miniature Oriental Rugs & Carpets *Meik & Ian McNaughton*
Needlepoint 1/12 Scale: Design Collections for the Dolls' House
Felicity Price
New Ideas for Miniature Bobbin Lace *Roz Snowden*
Patchwork Quilts for the Dolls' House: 20 Projects in 1/12 Scale
Sarah Williams
Simple Country Furniture Projects in 1/12 Scale *Alison J. White*
How to Make Your Dolls' House Special: Fresh Ideas for Decorating
Beryl Armstrong

Upholstery

Upholstery: A Complete Course (Revised Edition) *David James*
Upholstery Restoration *David James*
Upholstery Techniques & Projects *David James*
Upholstery Tips and Hints *David James*

MAGAZINES

WOODTURNING
WOODCARVING
FURNITURE & CABINETMAKING
THE ROUTER
NEW WOODWORKING
THE DOLLS' HOUSE MAGAZINE
OUTDOOR PHOTOGRAPHY
BLACK & WHITE PHOTOGRAPHY
TRAVEL PHOTOGRAPHY
MACHINE KNITTING NEWS
KNITTING
GUILD OF MASTER CRAFTSMEN NEWS

The above represents a selection of titles currently
published or scheduled to be published.
All are available direct from the Publishers or through
bookshops, newsagents and specialist retailers.

To place an order, or to obtain a complete catalogue, contact:

GMC PUBLICATIONS
166 HIGH STREET
LEWES
EAST SUSSEX
BN7 1XU
UNITED KINGDOM
TEL: 01273 488005
FAX: 01273 478606
E-MAIL: pubs@thegmcgroup.com

Orders by credit card are accepted.